ANALOGICAL MODELING OF LANGUAGE

ANALOGICAL MODELING OF LANGUAGE

ROYAL SKOUSEN

Department of English
Brigham Young University

KLUWER ACADEMIC PUBLISHERS
DORDRECHT / BOSTON / LONDON

Library of Congress Cataloging in Publication Data

Skousen, Royal.
Analogical modeling of language / Royal Skousen.
p. cm.
Includes bibliographical references (p.
ISBN 0-7923-0517-5 (U.S.)
1. Linguistic analysis (Linguistics) 2. Linguistic models.
I. Title.
P126.S57 1989
410--dc20 89-24539

ISBN 0-7923-0517-5

Published by Kluwer Academic Publishers,
P.O. Box 17, 3300 AA Dordrecht, The Netherlands.

Kluwer Academic Publishers incorporates
the publishing programmes of
D. Reidel, Martinus Nijhoff, Dr W. Junk and MTP Press.

Sold and distributed in the U.S.A. and Canada
by Kluwer Academic Publishers,
101 Philip Drive, Norwell, MA 02061, U.S.A.

In all other countries, sold and distributed
by Kluwer Academic Publishers Group,
P.O. Box 322, 3300 AH Dordrecht, The Netherlands.

Printed on acid-free paper

Printed in the Netherlands

To My Father

LEROY BENTLEY SKOUSEN

1917–1964

ACKNOWLEDGEMENTS

I would first like to thank Richard Cracroft, until recently the dean of the College of Humanities at Brigham Young University, for his encouragement and support of this book. I would also like to thank John B. Harris and Bert Wilson, past and present chairmen of the English Department, for their support, in particular the computer assistance I have received over the last few years. I am especially grateful for the year's research leave that I had during 1985-86. This time allowed me to concentrate on this project and write the computer programs. I would also like to thank my colleagues and fellow scholars in the College of Humanities, for their friendship and congeniality.

I am also very grateful to Bruce Derwing of the University of Alberta for his especially helpful review of the manuscript. His many suggestions have greatly helped to improve the readability of this book.

I would especially like to thank a number of people at Brigham Young University for help in typesetting the book: Jonathan Skousen, University Typographer; Willis Fails, Professor of Spanish and Portuguese; and Mel Smith, Faculty Computer Consultant at the Humanities Research Center. And the Department of Philosophy provided valuable technical assistance.

But of greatest importance, I must thank my wife, Sirkku. She never despaired or gave up hope – and she never let me give up. She saw the vision of it all. Truly, "an help meet" for me.

TABLE OF CONTENTS

ANALOGICAL MODELING OF LANGUAGE

INTRODUCTION

1. Structuralist Versus Analogical Descriptions

ONE important purpose of this book is to compare two completely different approaches to describing language. The first of these approaches, commonly called *structuralist*, is the traditional method for describing behavior. Its methods are found in many diverse fields – from biological taxonomy to literary criticism. A structuralist description can be broadly characterized as a system of classification. The fundamental question that a structuralist description attempts to answer is how a general contextual space should be partitioned. For each context in the partition, a rule is defined. The rule either specifies the behavior of that context or (as in a taxonomy) assigns a name to that context. Structuralists have implicitly assumed that descriptions of behavior should not only be correct, but should also minimize the number of rules and permit only the simplest possible contextual specifications. It turns out that these intuitive notions can actually be derived from more fundamental statements about the uncertainty of rule systems.

Traditionally, linguistic analyses have been based on the idea that a language is a system of rules. Saussure, of course, is well known as an early proponent of linguistic structuralism, as exemplified by his characterization of language as "a self-contained whole and principle of classification" (Saussure 1966:9). Yet linguistic structuralism did not originate with Saussure – nor did it end with "American structuralism". The Neogrammarian approach to historical change – "phonetic laws have no exception" – is clearly structuralist. And it must be recognized that Chomsky himself is a structuralist par excellence. His attack against American structuralists was not an attack against structuralism per se, but instead was an attack against some of the methodological assumptions that these linguists had espoused. For Chomsky (and virtually all other linguists today) there is no doubt that language is rule governed and that language behavior must be accounted for in terms of explicit rules. As a corollary, language acquisition is viewed as learning rules and language change as a change in the rules.

Nonetheless, a number of conceptual and empirical problems arise when we try to describe language in terms of rules. In order to eliminate these difficulties, this book introduces a new way of accounting for language behavior, one that can be called *analogical*. But unlike the imprecise and impressionistic appeals to "analogy" that have characterized language studies in the past, the analogical approach that this book proposes is based on an explicit definition of analogy. The main problem with traditional analogy is that there is no limit to its use: almost any form can be used to explain the behavior of another form, providing there is some similarity, however meager, between the two forms. Nor does this book use analogy to handle only the cases that the rules cannot account for. Instead, everything is considered analogical, even the cases of complete regularity.

Basically, an analogical description predicts behavior by means of a collection of examples called the *analogical set*. For a given context x, we construct the analogical set for x by looking through the data for (1) classes of examples that are the most similar to x and (2) more general classes of examples which behave like those examples most similar to x. The probability that a particular kind of occurrence will serve as the analogical model depends on several interrelated factors:

(1) the similarity of the occurrence to the given context x;

(2) the frequency of the occurrence; and

(3) whether or not there are intervening occurrences closer to x with the same behavior.

In many cases the predicted behavior is nearly the same no matter whether a rule approach or an analogical one is used, but conceptually the two approaches are vastly different. Some of the important differences between these two approaches are:

STRUCTURALIST APPROACH	ANALOGICAL APPROACH
a system of rules	an extensive data set derived from actual language data
based on types of behavior	based on tokens of behavior
contextual space is partitioned into rule contexts	contextual space remains atomistic
global, macroscopic	local, microscopic
need for a learning strategy to discover the rules from the data	need for a strategy to access the data set and analyze the data
static, rigid	dynamic, flexible
usage: find the correct rule that applies to the given context	usage: find an appropriate example to model behavior after
need to know how the rules interact	need to be able to access data quickly
transitions in predicted behavior ("boundaries") are sharp and precise	transitions in predicted behavior are gradual and fuzzy
rule governed	appears to be rule governed
general predictions can be made from rules alone	predictions can be made only in terms of given contexts
explicit, direct	implicit, indirect
usage is a function of the description	usage is the description

Many of these same distinctions are found in Winograd's notion of "declarative" versus "procedural" knowledge (Winograd 1975:185-191) or in Rumelhart's distinction between factual knowledge ("knowledge that") and procedural knowledge ("knowledge how") (Rumelhart 1979:2). Recent connectionist models of behavior share many procedural properties with analogical models. But as we shall see in the course of this book, there are significant differences between connectionist and analogical approaches to language.

This book concentrates on language, even though many of the results are applicable to more general kinds of behavior. Moreover, I do not discuss the properties of structuralism in any detail; and the underlying statistical basis for my analogical approach is only marginally considered in this book. These fundamental matters are taken up in my book *Analogy and Structure*. In that work (as yet unpublished) I discuss such topics as measures of uncertainty, optimality of rule descriptions, and the notion of natural statistics in analogical descriptions. *Analogy and Structure* is an important precursor to this book and I will occasionally summarize its findings in the following pages.

2. An Overview of the Book

CHAPTER 1: There are three kinds of behavior that a theory of language description must account for: (1) categorical, (2) exceptional/ regular, and (3) idiosyncratic. In order to help visualize the differences between these types, I first construct simple artificial examples of these three basic types of behavior. I also show how a rule approach would describe these basic types.

I then turn to the empirical and conceptual problems that rule approaches have. First of all, there is empirical evidence from language behavior that the boundaries between different types of behavior are not well-defined. I consider a number of examples from English: children's use of the indefinite article (*a/an*), misspellings, morphological extensions, pronunciation of nonce spellings, experiments with voicing onset time, and Labov's semantic experiments.

In addition, there are some conceptual problems with rule approaches. One particular difficulty is the indeterminacy that occurs when either no rule or more than one rule is applicable. Yet evidence from language usage clearly demonstrates that speakers can readily deal with cases of missing information and ill-formed contexts. In addition, rule approaches have difficulty in dealing with redundancy.

CHAPTER 2: I begin this chapter by giving an overview of how the analogical approach works. I then go through a step-by-step description of how to construct the analogical set for a given context. Important constructs are defined: data set, network of pointers, agreement and disagreement, uncertainty, given context, supracontext, homogeneity and heterogeneity, and rule of usage. One important result is that there is no need for the traditional methods of statistical analysis in order to determine contextual heterogeneity. Instead, I propose a very simple but powerful decision procedure that minimizes the number of disagreements. I also develop a few of the properties of analogical descriptions (such as the exponential effect in saturated deterministic fields of data).

At the end of the chapter, I apply the analogical approach to the three simple examples of categorical, exceptional/regular, and idiosyncratic behavior from chapter 1. The analogical approach captures the basic "rule governedness" of these examples, but also permits leakage across boundaries. In addition, I also briefly discuss the various factors that determine the slope of transition at boundaries. And in contrast to rule approaches, an analogical approach can readily handle cases of indeterminacy: behavior can be predicted even when the given context is either "ill-formed" or missing some "crucial" variable. In other words, an analogical approach predicts the kind of behavior that language actually exhibits.

CHAPTER 3: In this chapter I apply the analogical approach to several examples from English. I first discuss problems that arise when constructing the data set for language examples. Two important questions that must be considered are: (1) which variables should be represented in the data set; and (2) should the data set be based on token or type occurrences?

After considering these questions, I construct the data sets for three detailed examples. Each example represents one of the three basic types of behavior:

categorical	indefinite article
	a (followed by a consonant) *an* (followed by a vowel)
exceptional/regular	spelling of initial /h/ sound
	<h> regular case <wh> major exception <j> minor exception
idiosyncratic	categorization of labial stops (in terms of voicing onset time)
	/b/ [-107,2] milliseconds /p/ [51,94] milliseconds

In the categorical example, I show how leakage favors the more frequent outcome (that is, *a* rather than *an*) – not only during language acquisition, but also later. Moreover, an analogical approach can usually predict the appropriate form of the indefinite article even when the following segment is masked out by noise or is simply deleted. Whenever the crucial information is missing, the analogical approach uses a combination of redundancy and word recognition to make predictions about behavior.

While considering the exceptional/regular example, I discuss the notion of a gang effect and introduce an explicit definition for this effect. I also show how the gang effect measures the degree of regularity for any given context that actually occurs in the data. Typically, exceptional data occurrences have a gang effect of less than one, whereas regular data occurrences have a gang effect of greater than one.

Finally, in discussing the case of voicing onset time, I show how a continuous variable can be analyzed as a sequence of discrete variables. In addition, I consider how the number of variables affects the rate of transition across the empty contextual space between idiosyncratic occurrences.

CHAPTER 4: One of the most difficult problems in language description has been non-deterministic or probabilistic language behavior. Rule approaches typically account for such behavior by positing probabilistic rules. Even if we suppose that probabilities exist, there is still the very difficult question of how those probabilities are actually learned from the statistics and then used to predict behavior. But in an analogical approach no probabilities are directly postulated; instead, an analogical set of examples is constructed and then one of these examples is randomly selected in order to predict stochastic behavior. Thus it may look as if probabilities are learned, but in fact none are.

In this chapter I also discuss the connectionist models of behavior that have been proposed by McClelland and Rumelhart. Their activation model (now referred to as "parallel distributed processing") is another procedural alternative to declarative rule approaches. Yet there are some serious difficulties with McClelland and Rumelhart's model. I will argue that their approach cannot learn specific probabilities, nor can it adjust to alternative rules of usage or momentarily eliminate specific outcomes from consideration.

In the second half of this chapter, I consider how an analogical approach deals with multivariate data. If a given context actually occurs, the analogical prediction, it turns out, is not very interesting unless we introduce imperfect memory into our analogical approach. I then show that imperfect memory is equivalent to smaller, less powerful levels of statistical significance. Under conditions of imperfect memory an analogical approach can achieve all the statistical properties necessary for predicting multivariate behavior, but without any statistics!

In this chapter I apply the analogical method under conditions of imperfect memory to two examples of multivariate behavior: the well-known case of final-stop deletion in Black English and a complex case of sociolinguistic variation in colloquial Egyptian Arabic. I also consider some of the difficulties that have arisen when variationists have attempted to account for such complex cases of linguistic variation. The main problem here has been the inherent difficulty in describing variation by means of a system of rules, probabilistic or otherwise.

CHAPTER 5: In this chapter I show how the analogical approach deals with a complex case of historical drift in Finnish. There are a couple dozen Finnish verbs whose past tense forms originally ended in *si*, but which now end in *ti* in the standard language, yet there has been no systematic explanation of how this could have happened. In this chapter I first show how a restricted principle of homophone avoidance originally changed at least two past tense forms from *si* to *ti*. The effect of this minor change in an already sparse field was sufficient to break down the original gang effect of that field. Under conditions of imperfect memory, the analogical approach then predicts the subsequent historical drift, so that over time other verbs in this field have also changed their past tense forms from *si* to *ti*. The analogical approach thus accounts for the original instability of certain past tense forms in Finnish. It also predicts the overall stability of the past tense in the modern standard language.

CHAPTER 6: In this concluding chapter I consider the benefits of constructing the analogical set using massively parallel processing. And I also consider the parallels between the analogical approach in language and the atomistic approaches of physics.

APPENDICES: At the end of the book I include three appendices. The first lists the phonemic symbols for English that are used in this book. The second appendix gives five data sets that are used extensively in chapters 3 through 5: the indefinite article in English, the spelling of initial /h/ in English, the voicing distinction between /b/ and /p/ in English, terms of address in colloquial Egyptian Arabic, and past tense formation in Finnish. In the third appendix, I provide the computer program that I used to derive the results of this book. The parameters in this program are set so that the program will make analogical predictions for the data on final-stop deletion in Black English (as discussed in section 4.3).

Chapter One

PROBLEMS WITH RULE DESCRIPTIONS OF LANGUAGE

1. Three Basic Types of Language Behavior

A theory of language description must account for three types of language behavior: (1) categorical, (2) exceptional/regular, and (3) idiosyncratic. In this chapter we will first consider how a rule-based approach accounts for these three types of behavior. Then we will consider some of the empirical and conceptual problems with rule descriptions.

In this section we define three hypothetical data sets. In these examples there are two outcomes (*x* and *o*) and the behavior is deterministic. The symbol *U* stands for the general (or universal) contextual space. Arabic numerals are used to define three variables, allowing us to specify up to thirty-two fully-specified contexts in *U:*

VARIABLE	ALTERNATIVES
1	0, 1
2	2, 3, 4, 5
3	6, 7, 8, 9

In the categorical and exceptional/regular examples we specify twelve of these contexts; in the idiosyncratic example, we specify only two of these contexts:

CONTEXT	TYPE OF BEHAVIOR		
	categorical	exceptional/ regular	idiosyncratic
027	*x*	*o*	–
039	*x*	*o*	–
046	*x*	*o*	–
047	*x*	*x*	*x*
048	*x*	*o*	–
058	*x*	*o*	–
126	*o*	*o*	*o*
137	*o*	*o*	–
147	*o*	*o*	–
148	*o*	*o*	–
157	*o*	*o*	–
159	*o*	*o*	–

Graphically we may represent these data sets as follows:

(1) categorical behavior:

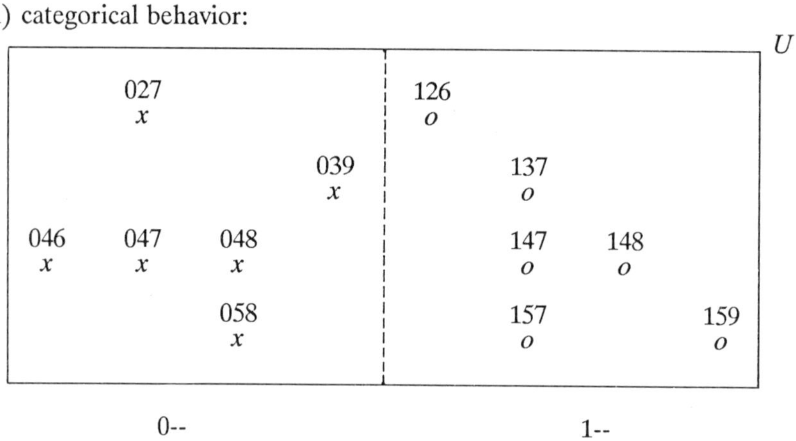

(2) exceptional/regular behavior:

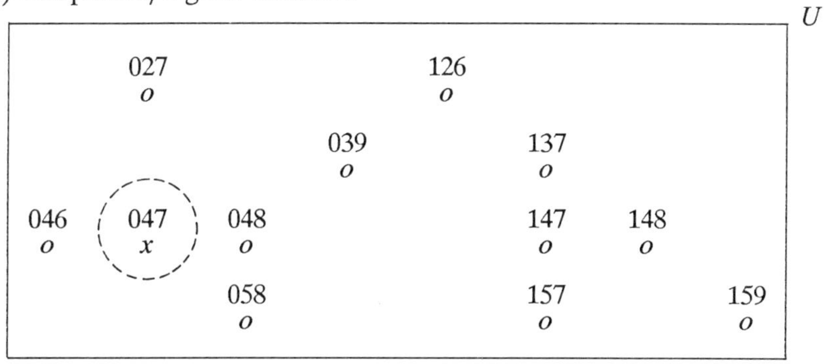

(3) idiosyncratic behavior:

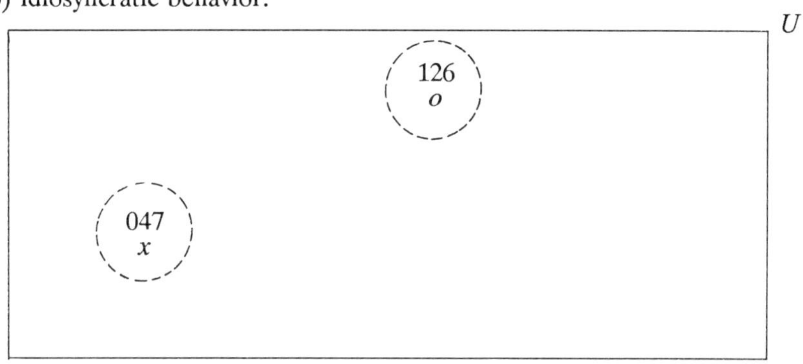

For each of these three data types, the rule description is quite simple:

categorical:	R_1	0-- $\rightarrow x$
	R_2	1-- $\rightarrow o$
exceptional/regular:	R_1	047 $\rightarrow x$
	R_2	$\overline{047} \rightarrow o$
idiosyncratic:	R_1	047 $\rightarrow x$
	R_2	126 $\rightarrow o$

In specifying the exceptional/regular behavior, we use a macron above the exceptional context 047 to stand for negation; that is, $\overline{047}$ stands for "not 047". Sometimes rule ordering can be used to further simplify rule specifications for exceptional/regular behavior:

$$\text{exceptional/regular:} \quad \left(\begin{array}{ll} R_1 & 047 \rightarrow x \\ R_2 & U \rightarrow o \end{array} \right.$$

Generally speaking, we attempt to write the simplest possible rule descriptions (providing they correctly describe the behavior of the data). We reject other rule descriptions that unnecessarily increase the number of symbols needed to describe the behavior correctly. For instance, another correct description of our categorical example would be the following:

$$\begin{array}{ll} R_1 & \text{02-} \rightarrow x \\ R_2 & \text{03-} \rightarrow x \\ R_3 & \text{04-} \rightarrow x \\ R_4 & \text{05-} \rightarrow x \\ R_5 & \bar{0}\text{--} \rightarrow o \\ R_6 & 147 \rightarrow o \end{array}$$

Of course, rules R_1 through R_4 miss "a significant generalization" and should be combined into a single rule, 0-- → x. Rule R_5 replaces the rule 1-- → o with a negatively defined context; that is, rule R_5 uses one additional mark, the negative macron. And the last rule, R_6, is completely unnecessary since it is a subrule of rule R_5.

A rule system alone cannot make any predictions about behavior unless we assign an empirical interpretation to the rules. In other words, we must specify how the rules are to be used to predict behavior.[1] We offer as a first approximation the following rule of usage:

---

[1] For additional discussion regarding the necessity of empirical interpretations, see my article "Empirical Interpretations of Psychological Reality" (Skousen 1979) or Derwing 1979 for his discussion of the "interpretation problem" – that is, "what *empirical claims*, if any, are to be associated with any particular linguistic description" (Derwing 1979:83).

> *When we wish to predict the behavior for a given context, we first find the rule context (if any) that contains the given context as a subcontext and predict that the behavior of the given context will be identical to the behavior of that rule context.*

For instance, the rules for the categorical behavior would predict that the outcome for a given 029 would be *x* since 029 is a subcontext of 0-- and the rule is 0-- → *x*. In the exceptional/regular example, 047 would have the predicted outcome *x* since the given context 047 is a subcontext of 047. (By definition, every context is a subcontext of itself.) On the other hand, 059 and 149 would have the predicted outcome *o* since 059 and 149 are not subcontexts of 047. In the idiosyncratic case, this rule of usage would predict the outcome for only a given 047 or 126.

2. *Empirical Problems*

UNFORTUNATELY, a rule approach to language description leads to a number of empirical and conceptual problems. Let us consider the empirical difficulties first. When the behavior is either categorical or exceptional/regular, the rules partition the general contextual space. In such a case, one important result of the rule of usage is that the predicted behavior at contextual boundaries is sharply demarcated:

PREDICTED BEHAVIOR

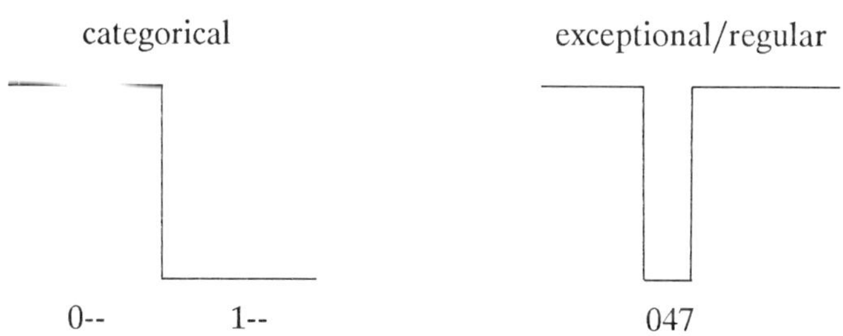

More problematic is the case of idiosyncratic behavior, when no contextual boundary can be unambiguously defined:

idiosyncratic

047 ? 126

Yet actual language behavior suggests fuzziness rather than sharp demarcation at boundaries and in empty spaces. We give a number of examples for each of our three kinds of behavior.

(1) Real language behavior often allows leakage across categories, sometimes predominating in one direction. Consider, for instance, the indefinite article (*a*/*an*) in English. The choice of *a* or *an* is categorically determined by whether the following word begins with a consonant (*a boy*) or a vowel (*an apple*). But in children's speech, there is a strong tendency to replace *an* with *a*, but rarely the opposite of *a* being replaced by *an*. Consider the following examples (with italics added):

from Fletcher 1985:

(a) Sophie: "I want it go in *a* upper." (line 225, page 137)
[age 3 years, 5 months, 15 days]

—

Fran (mother): "[The letter] A becomes *an* ... alligator."
Sophie: "What's *a* alligator?" (lines 73-74, page 203)
[age 3 years, 11 months, 15 days]

from Bloom, Lightbown, and Hood 1975:

(b) Eric [age 2 years, 1 month, 1 week]:
"This *a* end." (page 44)
"No, this *a* engine." (page 44)

(c) Kathryn [age 2 years, 2 weeks]:
"I wanta make *a* egg." (page 62)
"Where's *a* other one?" (page 67)

(2) When near exceptions, regularly behaving items sometimes take on the exceptional behavior.

misspellings:

a repeated misspelling from Gates (1937:72):
GREAD 'grade' (compare *great* /greit/)

from a list of children's errors provided by Thomas D. Horn:
INCHOIR 'inquire' (compare *choir* /kwair/)

an historical example:
whole, whore, whoop all had initial /h/ historically, not /hw/, but these <wh> spellings were caused by the exceptional spelling of *who* (hū < hō < hwō) (Scragg 1974:59)

morphological forms:

from my own collection of natural speech:
axen 'axes' (compare *ox/oxen*, a highly exceptional plural)

from an (unpublished) experiment in nonce forms by Leland Lester:
uxen, a commonly predicted plural form
for the singular nonce *ux*

vowel pronunciations in nonce words (Johnson and Venezky 1976:262):

<theat>	25%	/θεt/ (compare *threat*)
	5%	/ε/ in other <ea> examples: <yeath, brean, pleal, glead, feak>
<plood>	20%	/pləd/ (compare *blood, flood*)
	1%	/ə/ in other <oo> examples: <foon, nool, toom, yook, doot>
<smow>	80%	/smou/ (compare *snow, mow*)
	18%	/ou/ in other <ow> examples: <bown, drow, trowd, towd, pown>
<doub>	16%	/dəb/ (compare *double*)
	3%	/ə/ in other <ou> examples: <frout, thoup, loun, rouch, soud>
<thoup>	53%	/θup/ (compare *soup*)
	13%	/u/ in other <ou> examples: <doub, frout, loun, rouch, soud>

(3) In empty space between idiosyncratic occurrences, the predicted behavior is transitional.

voicing onset time experiments (perceptual tests between voiced and voiceless stops show a region of shifting towards the voiceless stops as voicing onset time is increased):

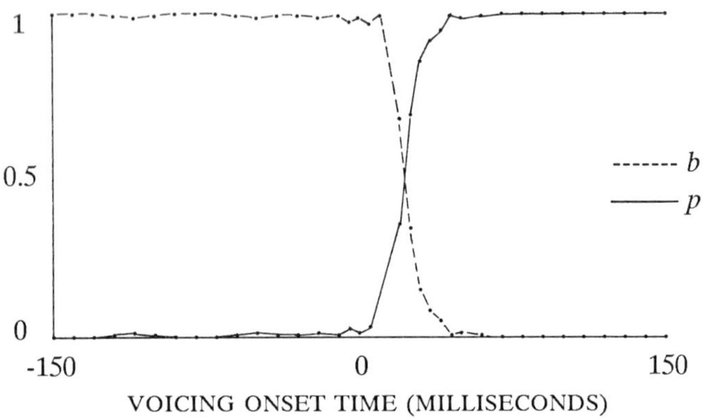

(adapted from Lisker and Abramson 1970:566)

semantic experiments (as the ratio of diameter to depth of a cup is increased, the greater the chances speakers will identify the cup as a bowl):

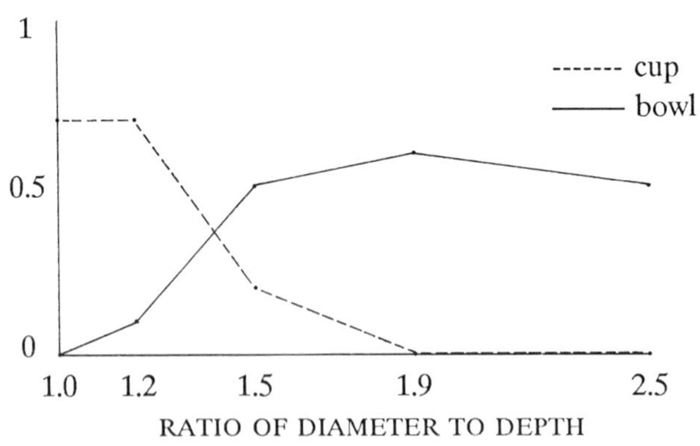

(adapted from Labov 1973:356)

3. Conceptual Problems

IN addition to the problem of fuzziness at boundaries, our rule of usage leads to various kinds of conceptual problems. These problems result from trying to partition the general contextual space. Let us consider once more our simple examples of the three basic types of language behavior from section 1. When we select various "odd" kinds of given contexts, our rule of usage fails. And in attempting to patch up this rule of usage, we discover that our desire for simple rule descriptions must be abandoned.

(1) *more than one rule context is applicable:*

Suppose the given context for the categorical behavior is $\rlap{0}1$37 – that is, the first variable is simultaneously 0 and 1. By our rule of usage, both rules 0-- → *x* and 1-- → *o* are applicable. In order to predict the outcome for this "deviant" or "ill-formed" given context, we need to revise our rule of usage to deal with cases when more than one rule is applicable. One possibility for revising our rule of usage is as follows:

> *We first identify all the applicable rules (using our previous rule of usage). Then we randomly select one of those applicable rules and predict behavior according to the outcome of that rule.*

Of course, if only one rule is applicable, then that rule will be chosen to predict the behavior of the given context.

(2) *no rule is applicable:*

Suppose the given context for the categorical behavior is either -37 or *A*37; that is, the first variable is either missing or something else (for example, *A*) has replaced the expected 0 or 1, with the result that neither rule 0-- → *x* nor rule 1-- → *o* is applicable. In other words, the given context is missing the "crucial" information. Now if we want our rule system to predict the behavior for this kind of given context, we must resign ourselves to allowing all sorts of "insignificant" rules in our description. For instance, in order to predict the behavior of -37 and

*A*37, we need at least one rule with the contextual specification -37, -3-, --7, or ---. In fact, this kind of problem implies that we may have to abandon our simplicity conditions on rule specifications.

(3) *problems with redundancy:*

Problems of non-unique rule applicability can also occur when the given context occurs in undefined contextual space. For instance, in the idiosyncratic rule system, the given context 036 occurs midway between the well-defined rule contexts 047 and 126. Neither rule context contains the given context as a subcontext, so no prediction can be made. But unlike the previous two problems, in this instance we could partially solve our problem by eliminating the redundancies in our rules. For instance, rule 047 → *x* could be replaced by six possibilities:

04- → *x*   0-7 → *x*   -47 → *x*   0-- → *x*   -4- → *x*   --7 → *x*

Similarly, rule 126 → *o* could be replaced by the following rules:

12- → *o*   1-6 → *o*   -26 → *o*   1-- → *o*   -2- → *o*   --6 → *o*

Yet depending on which redundancies might be eliminated, there would still be cases when either two or no rules would apply to our given context 036:

REVISED DESCRIPTIONS	PREDICTION
(i) 0-- → *x* --6 → *o*	contradictory 036: *x* or *o*
(ii) -4- → *x* 1-- → *o*	none 036: ø

Thus if we want rule systems to predict the behavior of non-normal given contexts, we must require (1) non-unique rule application and (2) overlapping, redundant rules. In the next chapter we will show how an analogical approach readily solves these conceptual problems.

There is, in fact, an abundance of evidence from language usage that would require our system of language description to handle these kinds of irregularities. Speakers can, for instance, readily deal with contexts in which the crucial information is missing. Consider, as an example, the following partially obscured word (McClelland and Rumelhart 1980, part I:24):

Even though the final letter is partially missing, it is obvious from what is given that the word must be *work*, not *word* nor the impossible *worr*. In a similar way, we can orthographically obscure all the vowel letters in sentences of English without seriously impairing our ability to understand what was intended, as in the following passage from Chomsky (1965:4):

> Th* pr*bl*m f*r th* l*ng**st, *s w*ll *s f*r th* ch*ld l**rn*ng th* l*ng**g*, *s t* d*t*rm*n* fr*m th* d*t* *f p*rf*rm*nc* th* *nd*rl**ng s*st*m *f r*l*s th*t h*s b**n m*st*r*d b* th* sp**k*r-h**r*r *nd th*t h* p*ts t* *s* *n *ct**l p*rf*rm*nc*.

In addition, speakers can interpret improperly formed sentences. Consider, for example, slips of the tongue like "John dropped his cuff of coffee" (Fromkin 1971:30) and ungrammatical sentences, including most of the starred sentences constructed by transformational grammarians (Jacobs and Rosenbaum 1968:4): "You don't can putting your feet on the table in here." We also note the difficulties of proofreading – typos and mispellings are often difficult to find.

Chapter Two

AN ANALOGICAL APPROACH

1. An Overview of the Analogical Model

THE easiest way to visualize the difference between a rule approach and an analogical one is to compare the two approaches in terms of rules. In a rule approach, when we wish to predict the behavior of a particular given context, we look for *the single rule* that applies to that context. Ideally, in a rule approach only one rule is applicable to a given context simply because a rule approach tries to partition the contextual space.

The analogical approach, on the other hand, is equivalent (from the perspective of a rule approach) to finding *all the rules* that can correctly apply to a given context. Not every possible rule can apply, but only those rules that are homogeneous in behavior. (A rule is homogeneous if all its subrules behave exactly like the rule itself.) In an analogical approach usually more than one rule is applicable to the given context, and these rules typically do not make the same prediction. Moreover, the rules are not all equally probable; rather, the probability of a particular rule being used turns out to be proportional to the square of the frequency of that rule.

Of course, the analogical approach does not actually use rules to predict behavior. Instead, the analogical approach (as its name suggests) makes predictions in terms of individual occurrences. Moreover, the fact that rule applicability in an analogical approach is proportional to the square of the rule frequency is not a primitive, but is derivable from general principles.

The first task of an analogical approach is to define a measure of uncertainty. The simplest measure of uncertainty is based on the number of disagreements between classes of data occurrences. The second task is to identify which data classes do not increase the number of disagreements. Such data classes are homogeneous in behavior. We then construct an analogical set from all the homogeneous data classes. Finally, we predict behavior by defining a rule of usage for the analogical set. In the following section, we consider a specific example and explicitly show how to measure uncertainty, determine homogeneity, construct the analogical set, and then apply a rule of usage in order to predict behavior.

2. *Constructing the Analogical Set for a Given Context*

WE now work through a simple artificial example to show precisely how our analogical approach predicts behavior. We always start with a *data set* – that is, a list of occurrences with each occurrence composed of a contextual specification plus an assigned outcome. In our artificial example, the context is specified by three variables, each of which can take on four variants:

VARIABLE	ALTERNATIVES
1	0, 1, 2, 3
2	0, 1, 2, 3
3	0, 1, 2, 3

The outcome for each occurrence has two possibilities, either *e* or *r* (where *e* stands for the "exceptional" outcome and *r* for the "regular" outcome). Our example data set is composed of the following five occurrences:

310*e*
032*r*
210*r*
212*r*
311*r*

The labeling *e* and *r* for the two outcomes is actually arbitrary. The terms "exceptional" and "regular" are externally imposed and only reflect the fact that there is but one data occurrence with the *e* outcome.

For this data set we define a *network of pointers*. We specify a pointer from each occurrence in the data set to every other occurrence, including itself:

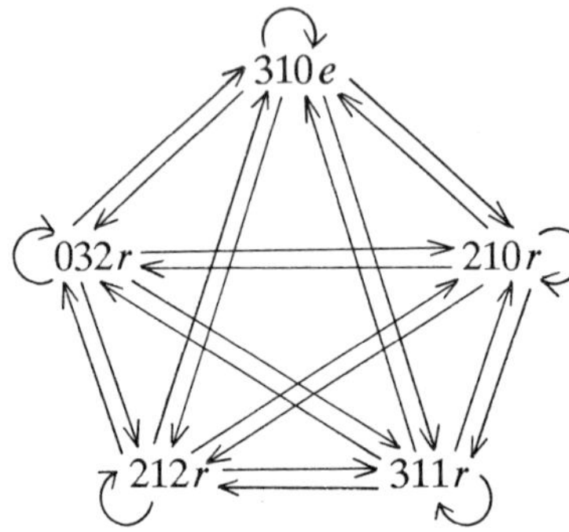

In this example, there are twenty-five pointers. In general, given n occurrences, there will be n pointers pointing to each occurrence, for a total of n^2. These pointers provide one-step access between data occurrences.

Now for each pointer in the network, we specify whether there is a change in outcome (a disagreement) or not (an agreement). Comparing our five occurrences in terms of their pointers, we observe the following:

310 → 310	*e,e*	same
310 → 032	*e,r*	different
310 → 210	*e,r*	different
310 → 212	*e,r*	different
310 → 311	*e,r*	different
032 → 310	*r,e*	different
032 → 032	*r,r*	same
032 → 210	*r,r*	same
032 → 212	*r,r*	same
032 → 311	*r,r*	same

210 → 310	*r,e*	different
210 → 032	*r,r*	same
210 → 210	*r,r*	same
210 → 212	*r,r*	same
210 → 311	*r,r*	same
212 → 310	*r,e*	different
212 → 032	*r,r*	same
212 → 210	*r,r*	same
212 → 212	*r,r*	same
212 → 311	*r,r*	same
311 → 310	*r,e*	different
311 → 032	*r,r*	same
311 → 210	*r,r*	same
311 → 212	*r,r*	same
311 → 311	*r,r*	same

The total number of disagreements is eight (out of a possible twenty-five):

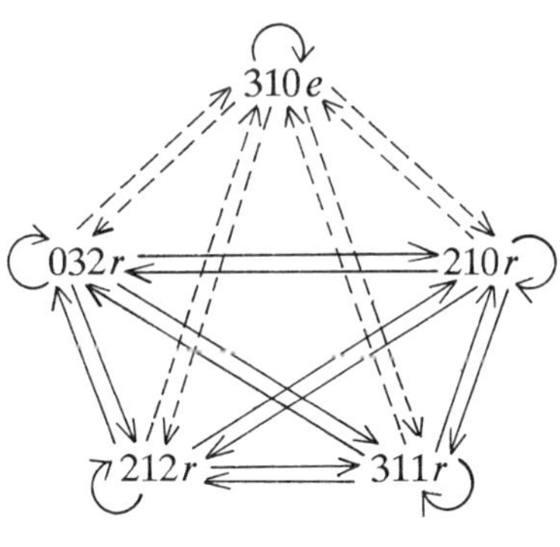

------- disagreement
—— agreement

We have the following general results (given I outcomes, n_i occurrences of outcome i (where $i = 1,\ldots,I$), and a total of n occurrences):

number of agreements for outcome *i:*	n_i^2
number of disagreements for outcome *i:*	$n_i(n - n_i)$
total number of agreements:	Σn_i^2
total number of disagreements:	$\Sigma n_i(n - n_i) = n^2 - \Sigma n_i^2$
total number of pairings:	n^2

From these values we define the *uncertainty* as the fraction of disagreement:

$$\Sigma n_i(n - n_i)/n^2 = (n^2 - \Sigma n_i^2)/n^2 = 1 - \Sigma (n_i/\mathrm{n})^2$$

Thus the uncertainty for our sample data set equals 8/25 (that is, 0.32):

number of agreements for outcome *e:* $1^2 = 1$
number of agreements for outcome *r:* $4^2 = 16$

number of disagreements for outcome *e:* $1(5 - 1) = 4$
number of disagreements for outcome *r:* $4(5 - 4) = 4$

total number of agreements: $1 + 16 = 17$
total number of disagreements: $4 + 4 = 8$
total number of pairings: $5^2 = 25 = 17 + 8$

uncertainty = fraction of disagreement: $8/25 = 0.32$

Now in an analogical approach, we can only predict behavior in terms of a *given context* – that is, a specified set of variables but without a specified outcome. For example, in our artificial example, we might be interested in predicting the outcome (*e* or *r*) for a given 312. To do this, we first determine all the contexts that contain the given context. We will refer to these contexts as the *supracontexts* of the given context. We determine these supracontexts by systematically eliminating the specified variables in the given context. In general, if there are m variables, there will be 2^m possible supracontexts.

Consider, for instance, our given context 312 and its supracontexts. We partition each supracontext into its subcontexts (as defined by the given context):

SUPRACONTEXT	SUBCONTEXTS
312	312
31-	312 $31\bar{2}$
3-2	312 $3\bar{1}2$
-12	312 $\bar{3}12$
3--	312 $3\bar{1}2$ $31\bar{2}$ $3\bar{1}\bar{2}$
-1-	312 $\bar{3}12$ $31\bar{2}$ $\bar{3}1\bar{2}$
--2	312 $\bar{3}12$ $3\bar{1}2$ $\bar{3}\bar{1}2$
---	312 $\bar{3}12$ $3\bar{1}2$ $31\bar{2}$ $\bar{3}\bar{1}2$ $\bar{3}1\bar{2}$ $3\bar{1}\bar{2}$ $\bar{3}\bar{1}\bar{2}$

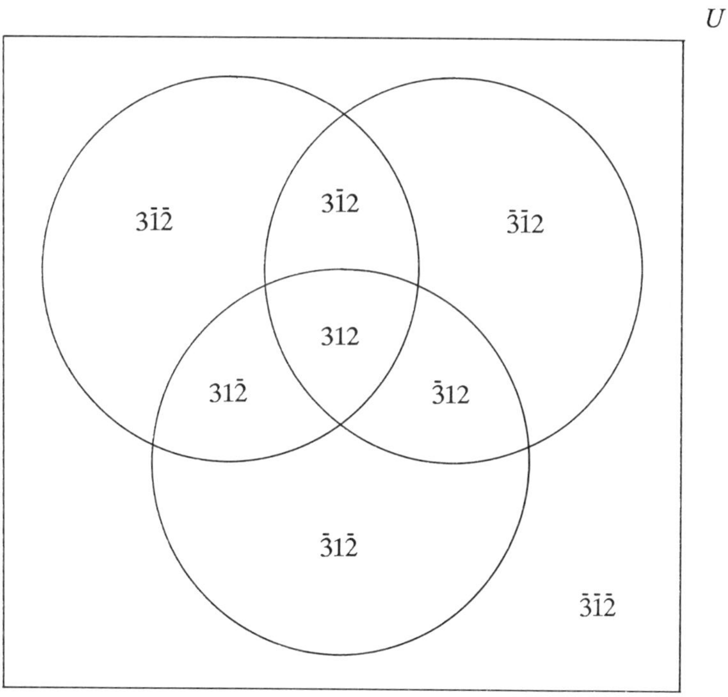

Now we count the number of disagreements in each of the subcontexts of a supracontext and compare the sum of these disagreements with the number of disagreements in the supracontext itself. To do this we first determine the number of disagreements in each of the subcontexts as defined by the given context:

SUBCONTEXT	BEHAVIOR	NUMBER OF DISAGREEMENTS
312	—	0
$31\bar{2}$	310*e* 311*r*	2
$3\bar{1}2$	—	0
$\bar{3}12$	212*r*	0
$3\bar{1}\bar{2}$	—	0
$\bar{3}1\bar{2}$	210*r*	0
$\bar{3}\bar{1}2$	032*r*	0
$\bar{3}\bar{1}\bar{2}$	—	0

In the following two diagrams we specify the behavior and the number of disagreements for each subcontext defined by the given context 312:

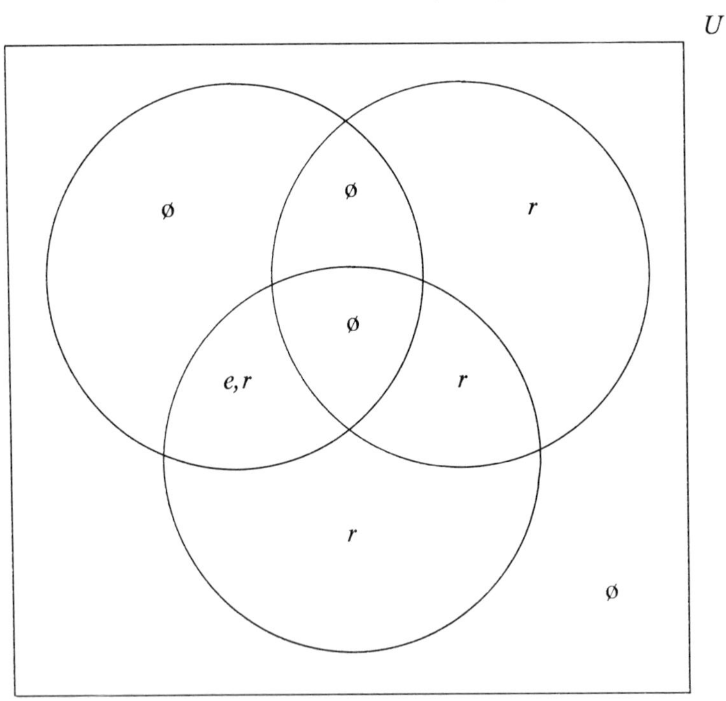

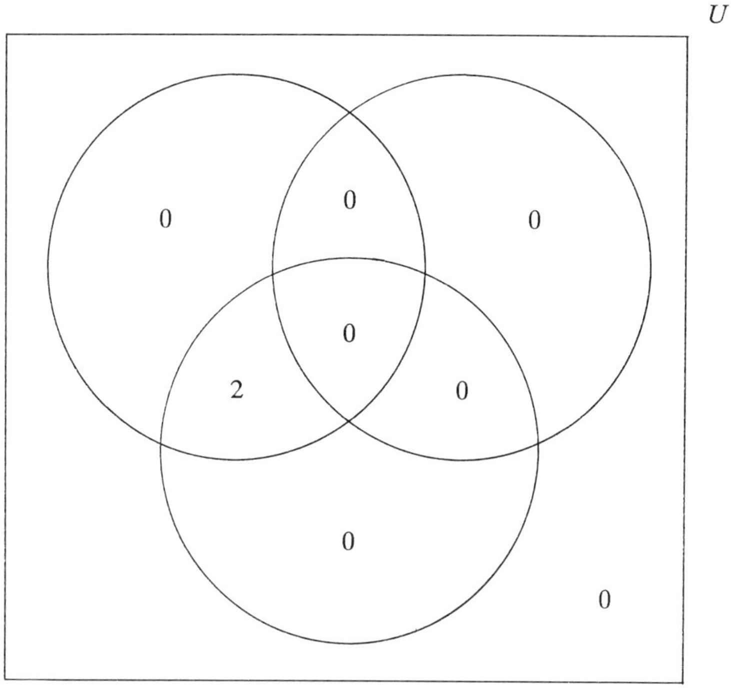

We note that only one subcontext (that is, $31\bar{2}$) has any disagreements – namely, two.

Using the formula for the total number of disagreements ($n^2 - \Sigma n_i^2$), we can construct a formula for determining the number of disagreements:

$$n^2 - n_r^2 - n_e^2 = 2n_r n_e,$$

where n_r is the number of regular occurrences, n_e the number of exceptional occurrences, and n the total number of occurrences ($n = n_r + n_e$). And using this formula we can calculate the number of disagreements for each supracontext and then compare that measure with the number of disagreements in its partition of subcontexts:

supracontextual analysis:

SUPRACONTEXT	DATA	DISAGREEMENTS
312	—	0
31-	310*e* 311*r*	2
3-2	—	0
-12	212*r*	0
3--	310*e* 311*r*	2
-1-	310*e* 210*r* 212*r* 311*r*	6
--2	212*r* 032*r*	0
---	310*e* 032*r* 210*r* 212*r* 311*r*	8

subcontextual analysis:

SUPRACONTEXT	SUBCONTEXTS	DISAGREEMENTS
312	312	0
31-	312 $31\bar{2}$	2
3-2	312 $3\bar{1}2$	0
-12	312 $\bar{3}12$	0
3--	312 $3\bar{1}2$ $31\bar{2}$ $3\bar{1}\bar{2}$	2
-1-	312 $\bar{3}12$ $31\bar{2}$ $\bar{3}1\bar{2}$	2
--2	312 $\bar{3}12$ $3\bar{1}2$ $\bar{3}\bar{1}2$	0
---	312 $\bar{3}12$ $3\bar{1}2$ $31\bar{2}$ $\bar{3}\bar{1}2$ $\bar{3}1\bar{2}$ $3\bar{1}\bar{2}$ $\bar{3}\bar{1}\bar{2}$	2

Since $31\bar{2}$ is the only subcontext with any disagreements, only those supracontexts containing $31\bar{2}$ will have any disagreements.

Comparing our two analyses, we notice that for only two supracontexts (-1- and ---) there is a difference in the number of disagreements. For the other six supracontexts, the number of disagreements is the same:

SUPRACONTEXT	SUBCONTEXTUAL DISAGREEMENTS	SUPRACONTEXTUAL DISAGREEMENTS
312	0	0
31-	2	2
3-2	0	0
-12	0	0
3--	2	2
-1-	2	6
--2	0	0
---	2	8

We now set up a very simple rule for determining supracontextual heterogeneity:

> *If there is an increase in the number of disagreements (in going from the subcontexts to the supracontext), then we say that the supracontext is* heterogeneous; *if the number of disagreements does not change, then the supracontext is* homogeneous.

For our artificial given context (312), we can identify three types of homogeneous supracontexts:

(1) *the supracontext is empty* (the given context 312 as well as 3-2)

Since an empty supracontext has no occurrences (and thus no pointers), there is no possibility of any disagreement in an empty supracontext. As a consequence, there can be no increase in the number of disagreements and the supracontext is trivially homogeneous.

3-2 (which contains 312)

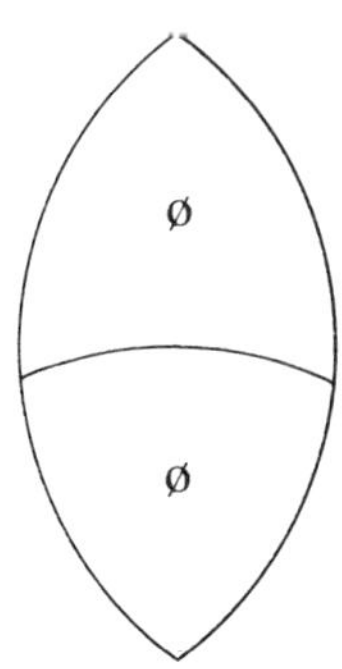

(2) *the supracontext is deterministic* (-12, --2)

Only one type of outcome occurs in the supracontext.

--2 (which contains -12)

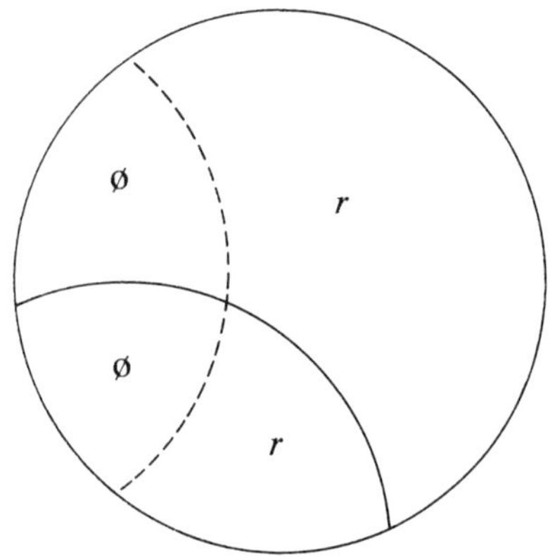

(3) *only one subcontext in the supracontext is non-empty* (31-, 3--, and -12)

The behavior of the one occurring subcontext may be either deterministic or non-deterministic. Since deterministic supracontexts are always homogeneous (see just above), we will ignore -12 and only list the non-deterministic homogeneous supracontexts under this type.

3-- (which contains 31-)

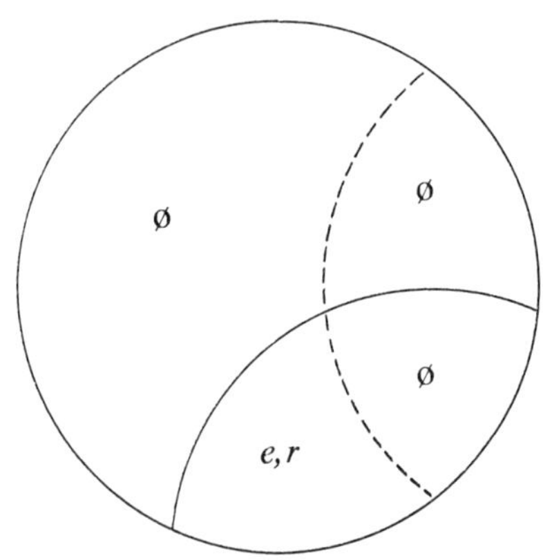

Ignoring the first type of homogeneous supracontext (the empty case), we can say that there are two basic types of homogeneous supracontexts:

(i) either the supracontext is deterministic or
(ii) the supracontext is unobstructed and non-deterministic.

By *unobstructed* we mean either that the single subcontext that occurs is the given context or that all the subcontexts between that single subcontext and the given context (including the given context) are empty. In 31- and 3-- the non-empty subcontext is 31$\bar{2}$; and the only subcontext closer to the given context (312) is 312 itself, which is empty.

The only two heterogenous supracontexts are -1- and ---. In each case the non-deterministic subcontext 31$\bar{2}$ is combined with a subcontext containing only the *r* outcome, thus leading to heterogeneity.

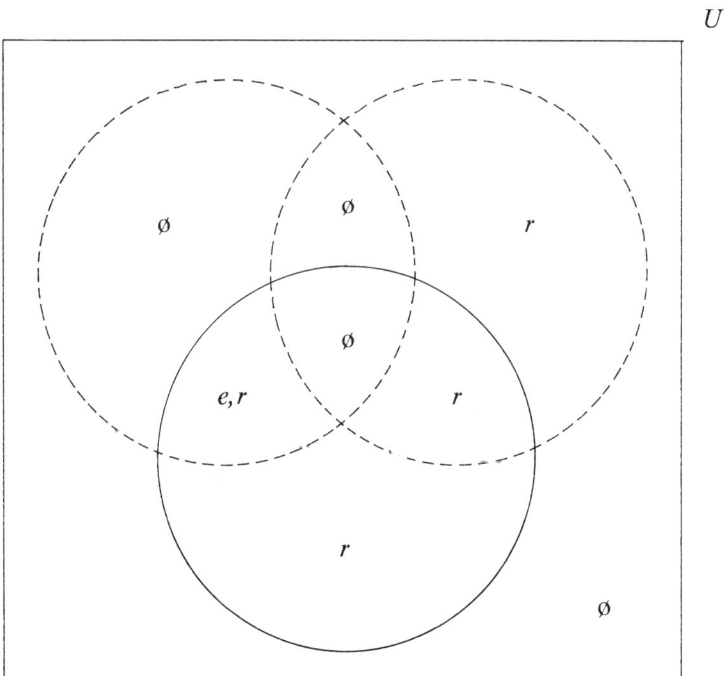

--- (which contains -1-)

We can automatically determine the heterogeneity of the general supracontext (---) simply because it contains a heterogeneous supracontext (-1-). In other words, having determined that a supracontext is heterogeneous, any more general supracontext containing that supracontext will also be heterogeneous. We refer to such cases as *inclusive heterogeneity*.

We now determine the statistical properties of our definition of heterogeneity. It turns out that our decision rule of never increasing the number of disagreements is equivalent to the most powerful statistical test possible. To see this, let us reinterpret the behavior of a supracontext and its subcontexts in terms of an $I \times J$ two-way contingency table:

	OUTCOMES				
	1	2	. . .	J	
SUBCONTEXTS					
1	n_{11}	n_{12}	. . .	n_{1J}	n_{1+}
2	n_{21}	n_{22}	. . .	n_{2J}	n_{2+}
⋮	⋮	⋮		⋮	⋮
I	n_{I1}	n_{I2}	. . .	n_{IJ}	n_{I+}
SUPRACONTEXT	n_{+1}	n_{+2}	. . .	n_{+J}	n

We can measure the divergence from identical behavior (or homogeneity) for this array in terms of Pearson's X^2, a standard statistical measure of divergence:

$$X^2 = n(\Sigma\Sigma(n_{ij}{}^2/n_{i+}n_{+j}) - 1)$$

The most powerful test for heterogeneity has a level of significance equal to one and occurs when Pearson's $X^2 = 0$. Setting $X^2 = 0$ is equivalent to saying that a supracontext is homogeneous only when every subcontext of the supracontext behaves *exactly* like that supracontext. This requirement leads to four possible cases:

(1) The supracontext is empty.

(2) The supracontext is deterministic in behavior (only one type of outcome occurs).

(3) The supracontext is non-deterministic in behavior (more than one type of outcome occurs), but only one subcontext actually occurs, so that the behavior of this subcontext is identical to the behavior of the supracontext itself.

(4) The supracontext is non-deterministic in behavior and more than one subcontext occurs, yet for each subcontext the relative frequency of outcomes is identical (that is, $n_{ij}/n_{i+} = n_{+j}/n$ for each occurring subcontext i and outcome j).

Our definition of supracontextual homogeneity is identical to the first three cases. But the fourth case is excluded. We can motivate this exclusion on the following grounds:

(i) The fourth case is the only one in which some arithmetic calculation is required; in the other three cases we need only consult the behavior of the margins. By eliminating this case our test for homogeneity actually becomes statistically free. We can thus determine homogeneity by simple inspection.

(ii) The fourth case represents a case of *potential heterogeneity*. Even if a non-deterministic supracontext is in fact homogeneous, the chances of its occurring subcontexts behaving exactly like the supracontext are extremely small. Thus the fourth case can be considered an unlikely possibility. We can therefore eliminate this case without unduly affecting the predicted behavior.

We now construct the *analogical set* for the given context. The analogical set contains all the pointers and their associated outcomes from each of the homogeneous supracontexts of the given context.

HOMOGENEOUS SUPRACONTEXT	OCCURRENCES WITH POINTERS	NUMBER OF POINTERS *e*	*r*
31-	310*e* ⇄ 311*r*	2	2
-12	212*r*	0	1
3--	310*e* ⇄ 311*r*	2	2
--2	212*r* ⇄ 032*r*	0	4
	totals	4	9

Thus four out of the thirteen pointers in the analogical set point to the exceptional outcome *e;* the remaining nine pointers are associated with the regular outcome *r.*

We note that a given pointer and its associated outcome may occur more than once in the analogical set. For instance, in our example, the occurrences 310*r,* 311*r,* and 212*r* occur in more than one homogeneous supracontext and thus their effect on the analogical set is greater than other occurrences:

OCCURRENCE	DISTANCE FROM GIVEN	NUMBER OF HOMOGENEOUS SUPRACONTEXTS	NUMBER OF POINTERS
310*e*	1	2	4
311*r*	1	2	4
212*r*	1	2	3
032*r*	2	1	2
210*r*	2	0	0

Having determined the analogical set for a given context, we now use the following *rule of usage* to predict the behavior of that given context:

random selection: *randomly select one of the pointers in the analogical set and predict behavior according to the outcome associated with that pointer.*

Using this rule of usage, the probability that the predicted outcome will be exceptional (that is, *e*) is 4/13 or 30.8%. The given context (312) is close to the exceptionally behaving 310*e*. Nonetheless, the regular behavior predominates: *Pr*(*r*) = 9/13 or 69.2% (where *Pr* stands for probability).

For each occurrence we can determine its *analogical effect* – namely, the probability that the predicted behavior will be due to that occurrence:

OCCURRENCE	NUMBER OF POINTERS	ANALOGICAL EFFECT (%)
310*e*	4	30.8
311*r*	4	30.8
212*r*	3	23.1
032*r*	2	15.4
210*r*	0	0

3. *The Exponential Effect in a Saturated Deterministic Field*

IN this section we apply our analogical approach to a saturated deterministic data set. (A data set is *saturated* if it contains at least one occurrence for every possible contextual specification.) When we construct the analogical set for a saturated deterministic data set, we find that the probability of an occurrence being used analogically is an exponential function of its distance from the given context. (Here the term "distance" refers to how far away an occurrence is from the given context; that is, the distance equals the number of disagreeing variables between the occurrence and the given context.)

Consider the following example in which the occurrences in the data set are defined by eight variables, each with two alternatives (0 and 1). The data set is saturated because all 256 possible occurrences are actually found in the data set. In addition, the data set is deterministic since all 256 occurrences have the same outcome (x):

DATA SET	00000000x	00000001x	00000010x	...
	11111101x	11111110x	11111111x	

For a given context we construct the analogical set and then determine how many pointers point to any particular occurrence in the data set. In this way we can determine for the given context the analogical effect of each occurrence in the data set. In a saturated deterministic field of n variables, if a particular occurrence has y variables in common with the given context, then the number of pointers in the analogical set pointing to that occurrence equals the following sum:

$$\sum_{0}^{y} \binom{y}{i} 2^{n-i}$$

The analogical effect for a particular occurrence is therefore an exponential function of the distance between that occurrence and the given context. We can see this in the following example where the given context is 00000000:

DISTANCE	SAMPLE OCCURRENCE	NUMBER OF POINTERS
0	00000000	6561
1	00000001	4374
2	00000011	2916
3	00000111	1944
4	00001111	1296
5	00011111	864
6	00111111	576
7	01111111	384
8	11111111	256

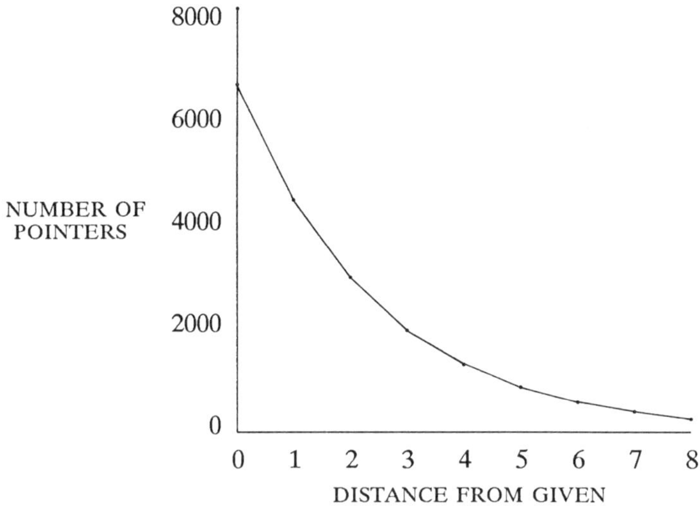

On the other hand, given a saturated idiosyncratic field (that is, every occurrence has a different outcome), only the occurrences contained in the given context are in the analogical set – and each of these occurrences has an equal probability of being selected as the analogical model. Suppose we have the same data set as above except that now there are 256 distinct outcomes (referred to as $x_0, \ldots, x_{255}$), a different one for each occurrence. As can be seen from the following examples, no occurrence (or its unique outcome) occurs more than once in any analogical set:

GIVEN CONTEXT	ANALOGICAL SET			
00000000	$00000000x_0$			
0000000-	$00000000x_0$	$00000001x_1$		
000000--	$00000000x_0$	$00000001x_1$	$00000010x_2$	$00000011x_3$
00000---	$00000000x_0$	$00000001x_1$	$00000010x_2$	$00000011x_3$
	$00000100x_4$	$00000101x_5$	$00000110x_6$	$00000111x_7$

Thus uniformity of behavior leads to an exponential effect, but diversity of behavior works to eliminate any possible exponential effect.

4. Predicting the Three Basic Behaviors Analogically

WE now apply our analogical approach to the three examples in chapter 1 to show the predicted behavior of our three basic types.

CATEGORICAL BEHAVIOR (0-- → *x*, 1-- → *o*)

data:	027*x*	039*x*	046*x*	047*x*	048*x*	058*x*
	126*o*	137*o*	147*o*	148*o*	157*o*	159*o*

predicted probability (in percent) of outcome *x*:

GIVEN CONTEXT	PREDICTED PROBABILITY	GIVEN CONTEXT	PREDICTED PROBABILITY
026	97.4	126	0
027	100	127	2.1
028	100	128	0
029	100	129	0
036	100	136	0
037	97.6	137	0
038	100	138	0
039	100	139	2.6
046	100	146	2.4
047	100	147	0
048	100	148	0
049	100	149	0
056	100	156	0
057	97.6	157	0
058	100	158	2.4
059	97.4	159	0

We see from these results that the predicted behavior of the data is basically categorical. The only time we get any "leakage" across the 0/1 "boundary" is when the given context 0*pq* does not occur, but 1*pq* does – or, conversely, when 1*pq* does not occur but 0*pq* does. (Here *p* and *q* are general symbols that stand for the other two variables). For instance, the non-occurring given context 026 is close to the occurring 126, which takes the *o* outcome. But even in these cases, the supracontexts 0-- and 1-- dominate and the leakage is only slight.

Overall, the analogically predicted behavior looks categorical. When the first variable is 0, the probability of getting the outcome *x* is 99.4%. On the other hand, when the first variable is 1, the probability of getting the outcome *x* is only 0.6%. The overall probability that the analogical prediction will differ from the rule prediction is only 0.6%. And this result is based on a data set of only twelve occurrences. Thus an analogical approach can readily capture the categorical behavior of a data set without resorting to a rule analysis. But it also predicts some slight fuzziness along the 0/1 "boundary".

We can get an idea of how quickly the analogical approach can "learn" or "discover" categorical behavior by setting up a random sequence of the thirty-two possible occurrences of this behavior:

1	2	3	4	5	6	7	8
047*x*	027*x*	058*x*	157*o*	126*o*	046*x*	137*o*	039*x*
9	10	11	12	13	14	15	16
148*o*	159*o*	048*x*	147*o*	056*x*	127*o*	029*x*	037*x*
17	18	19	20	21	22	23	24
129*o*	038*x*	136*o*	128*o*	138*o*	146*o*	059*x*	026*x*
25	26	27	28	29	30	31	32
028*x*	156*o*	057*x*	049*x*	149*o*	036*x*	139*o*	158*o*

(The first twelve occurrences are identical to our original categorical data set in chapter 1.) Now as we steadily increase our data set from only the first occurrence (047*x*) to all thirty-two occurrences, it is easy to see that the categorical behavior of the data has been essentially "discovered" by the time nine occurrences are found in the data set. (At nine occurrences, the overall leakage permanently drops below two percent.) Here we give the overall leakage (the probability of predicting the "wrong" outcome) as we increase the data:

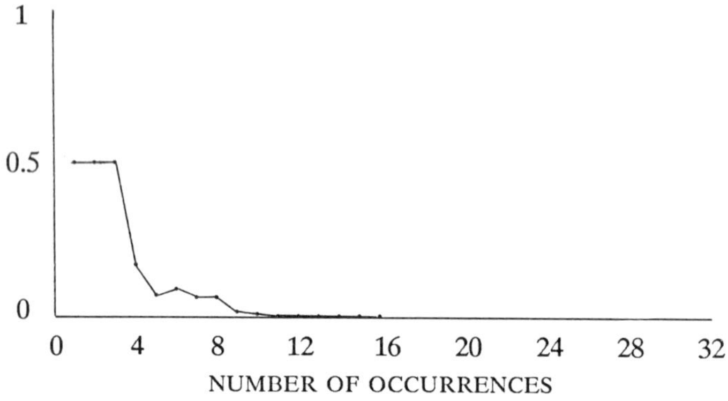

In a similar way, we can calculate the leakage for the categorical contexts, 0-- and 1--:

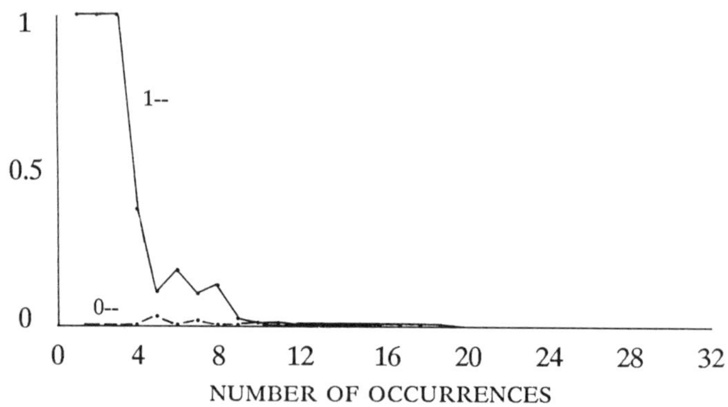

Or we can calculate the leakage for any fully-specified given context, such as 146, and identify which particular occurrences cause significant shifts in its predicted behavior:

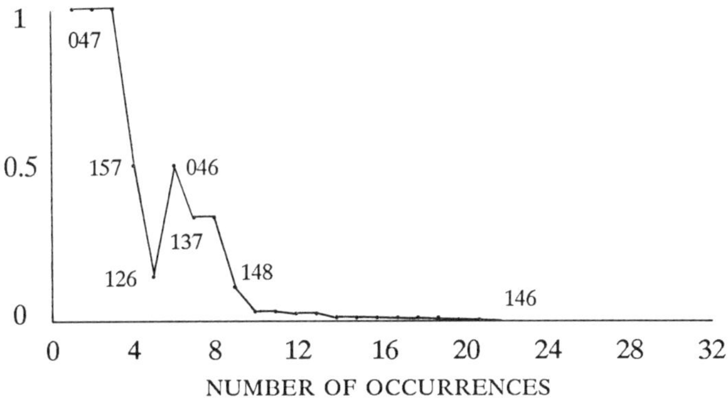

More importantly, an analogical approach can readily handle those "odd" kinds of given contexts mentioned in chapter 1. Consider first the "ill-formed" given context ⦶37, where the first variable is simultaneously 0 and 1. As before, we systematically analyze the occurring variables in order to determine the applicable supracontexts:

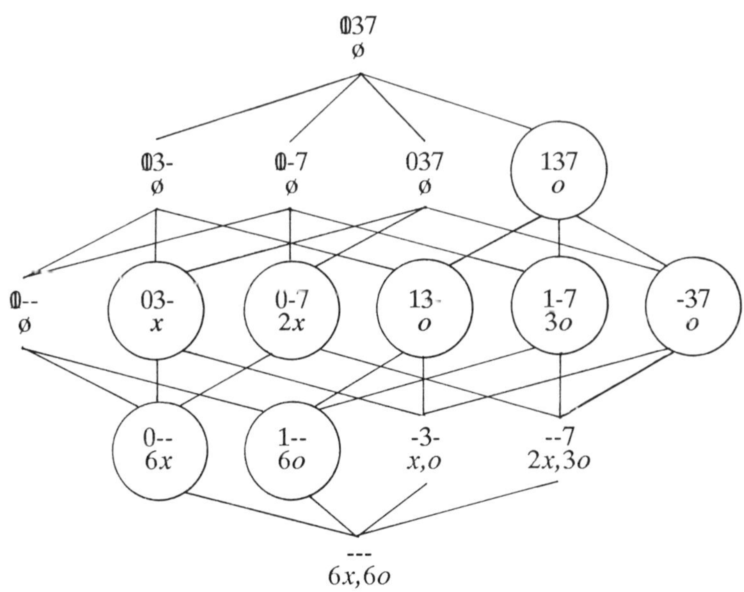

In this diagram, each interconnecting line represents a subcontextual relationship (for example, 137 is a subcontext of 13-). The non-empty homogeneous supracontexts are circled and form the analogical set:

HOMOGENEOUS SUPRACONTEXTS	NUMBER OF POINTERS	
	x	*o*
137	0	1
03-	1	0
0-7	4	0
13-	0	1
1-7	0	9
-37	0	1
0--	36	0
1--	0	36
totals	41	48

Thus the probability of predicting the *o* outcome is 48/89 = 53.9%. This slight favoring of the *o* outcome is because 137 occurs in the data set, but 037 does not. Nonetheless, the predicted behavior is nearly equal because of the dominating categorical behavior of the first variable (0/1).

This analogical approach also readily handles those given contexts from chapter 1 in which the crucial variable is missing. Consider first the given context -37, where the categorical variable 0/1 is missing. Here the prediction is rather simple:

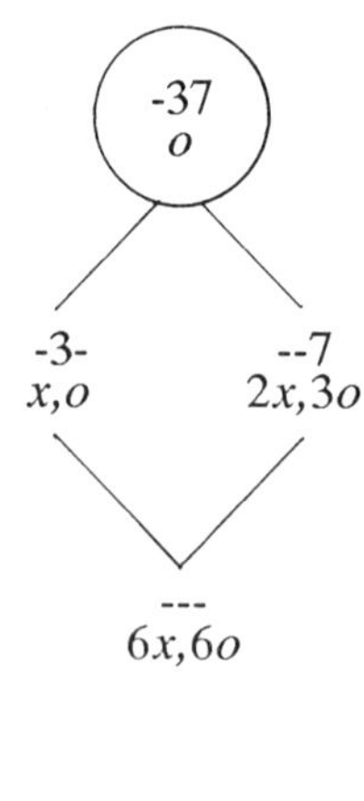

Only the *o* outcome is predicted. This is because the given context -37 is essentially interpreted as an occurrence of 137. When the crucial variable is missing, the analogical approach often uses a form of "word recognition" in order to predict the behavior of such a given context.

The same prediction is made when the crucial variable is replaced by something other than 0 or 1 (for example, *A*):

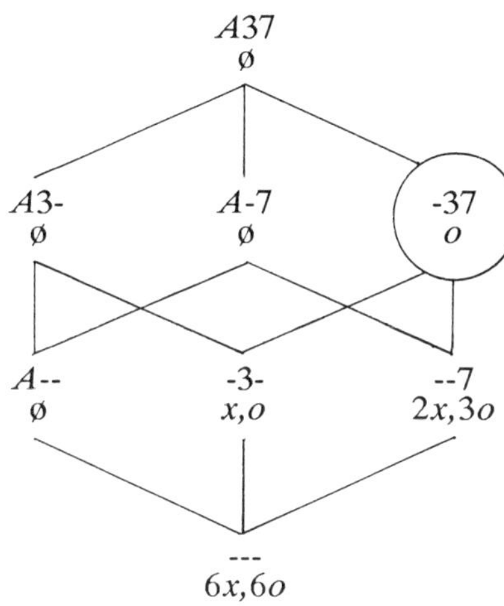

It makes no difference whether the crucial variable is missing (-) or masked by noise (*A*). But when both alternatives of the crucial variable occur (as in the given context 037), then we get a different prediction. In such a case, the analogical approach does not ignore the crucial variable; instead, it separates out the simultaneous variants and analyzes each one individually.

EXCEPTIONAL/REGULAR BEHAVIOR (047 → *x*, $\overline{047}$ → *o*)

data:	027*o*	039*o*	046*o*	047*x*	048*o*	058*o*
	126*o*	137*o*	147*o*	148*o*	157*o*	159*o*

predicted probability (in percent) of outcome *x:*

GIVEN CONTEXT	PREDICTED PROBABILITY	GIVEN CONTEXT	PREDICTED PROBABILITY
026	0	126	0
027	0	127	0
028	0	128	0
029	0	129	0
036	0	136	0
037	20.0	137	0
038	0	138	0
039	0	139	0
046	0	146	0
047	100	147	0
048	0	148	0
049	21.4	149	0
056	0	156	0
057	13.3	157	0
058	0	158	0
059	0	159	0

The analogically predicted behavior of this data is nearly exceptional/regular. The overall leakage is only 1.7%; in only three cases (037, 049, and 057) do we get some leakage towards exceptional behavior. In each of these cases, the given context is non-occurring and close to the exceptionally behaving 047. Nonetheless, regular behavior is still favored for these three cases; the regularly behaving occurrences work together to overwhelm the isolated 047. Thus once more the analogical prediction looks rule governed, with only some minor fuzziness occurring at the "boundary" between regular and exceptional behavior.

As in the example of categorical behavior, we can show how quickly the exceptional/regular behavior is "learned" or "discovered" by considering the analogical predictions as the data set is steadily increased from a single occurrence to all thirty-two. Here we assume that the first occurrence is the exceptional 047*x* (since no exceptional behavior can be predicted at all until 047*x* is in the data set). Overall, the data set only needs eleven regularly behaving occurrences in addition to the exceptional 047 for the exceptional/regular behavior to be "discovered" (at a permanent level of less than two percent leakage):

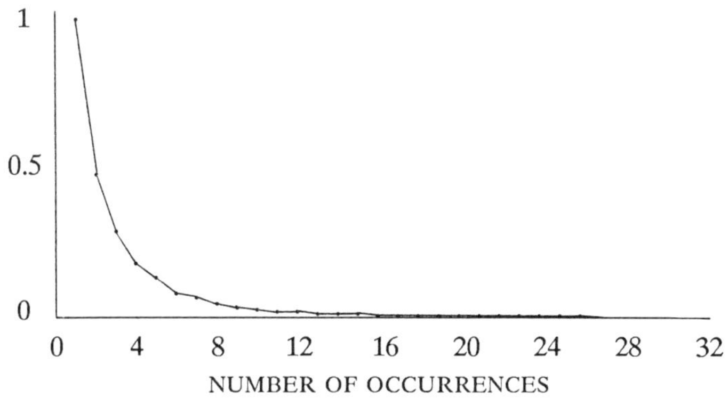

We can also calculate the leakage for given contexts according to their distance (*d*) from the exceptionally behaving 047:

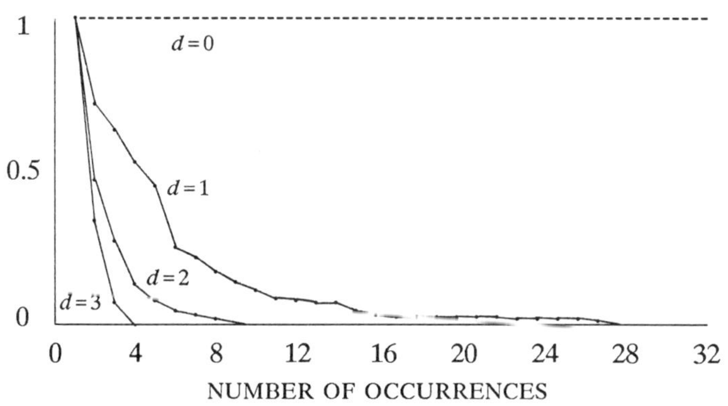

We see from this that only those given contexts right next to the exceptional 047 (that is, $d = 1$) are able to maintain a small probability of behaving exceptionally. Of course, even here the regular behavior soon dominates. And other supracontexts further away ($d > 1$) will eventually be surrounded by a field of regularity, so that given enough data these given contexts will not take on exceptional behavior.

IDIOSYNCRATIC BEHAVIOR (047 → *x*, 126 → *o*)

data: 047*x* 126*o*

predicted probability (in percent) of outcome *x*:

GIVEN CONTEXT	PREDICTED PROBABILITY	GIVEN CONTEXT	PREDICTED PROBABILITY
026	25	126	0
027	75	127	25
028	50	128	0
029	50	129	0
036	50	136	0
037	100	137	50
038	100	138	0
039	100	139	0
046	75	146	25
047	100	147	75
048	100	148	50
049	100	149	50
056	50	156	0
057	100	157	50
058	100	158	0
059	100	159	0

We note that the analogical approach readily predicts the behavior for any of the thirty-two fully-specified given contexts, not just the two that actually occur (047 and 126). The problem with redundancy that arose in chapter 1 (when we attempted to use a rule system to predict the behavior of 036) no longer exists. In an analogical approach there is no need to discover which rule variables are redundant.

For those given contexts that are directly between the two data points 047 and 126, we get a transition from *x* to *o* as we move from 047 to 126. We determine the predicted probability (in percent) of outcome *x* for proportional distances of one third and two thirds of the way from 047 to 126:

PROPORTIONAL DISTANCE	PREDICTED PROBABILITY
0/3 (047)	100
1/3 (046 027 147)	75
2/3 (026 146 127)	25
3/3 (126)	0

In this example, there are only three variables. As we increase the number of variables, the transition in predicted behavior becomes considerably sharper:

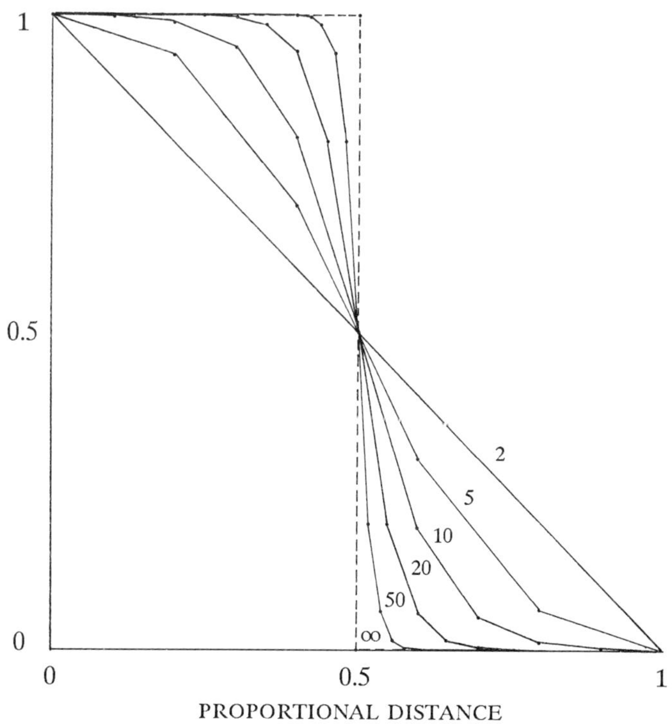

We get an abrupt shift in behavior only when the number of variables is infinite. Thus there will always be some areas of transitional behavior in a non-saturated non-uniform contextual space.

Finally, we should note that the analogical approach itself does not actually differentiate between these various types of behavior. For instance, if there were only two occurrences, 047*x* and 027*o,* in the exceptional/regular data set, there would be no difference at all between this data set and an idiosyncratic one (or even a categorical one in which the second variable determines the outcome). In other words, the transition from one type of behavior to another is not well-defined. (In fact, there can be data sets that are a mixture of categorical, exceptional/regular, and idiosyncratic behavior.) Moreover, there is no point at which the analogical approach actually "discovers" that the data behaves according to one of these types. Nonetheless, an analogical approach will eventually predict behavior as if it has somehow learned rules of some kind, but without any of the problems inherent in rule systems. Conceptually, an analogical approach makes the right kind of predictions.

Chapter Three

THREE EXAMPLES FROM ENGLISH

1. Specifying the Data Set

IN applying the analogical approach to actual language examples, we need to consider a number of questions on how to construct the data set. We must first select the variables that will specify the occurrences in the data set. We must also decide whether the data should be represented by token or by type.

The problem of variable selection results in part from a computational limit on the number of variables. If a given context has n variables, the number of supracontexts that must be considered is 2^n, an exponential function of n. In addition, the running time for the computer program that determines the analogical set is also a function of 2^n. Because of memory limitations (of 640 KB) on the computer used for calculating the analogical sets for this book, the maximum number of variables that could be specified was about eleven or twelve (depending on the number of occurrences in the data set itself). The running time, on the other hand, was never a limiting factor since the longest running time was no more than two minutes.

This problem with the number of variables can be alleviated – but never eliminated. By using inclusive heterogeneity, we can substantially reduce the number of supracontexts for which heterogeneity must be determined. In addition, we can store the results of previously determined homogeneous supracontexts, so that we need not construct the whole analogical set directly from the original data set each time we desire to predict the behavior of a given context. And ultimately, by means of massively parallel processing, the running time (but not the hardware requirements) can be reduced to a function of n rather than 2^n. (In the last chapter I show how parallel processing can achieve this significant decrease in running time.)

This limitation on the number of variables requires us to consider an important question: namely, which variables should be selected? In general, I have tried to select enough variables so that each occurrence in the data set is distinguishable or recognizable. For example, in order to predict the spelling of the initial /h/ sound in English (see section 3.3), I have defined twelve variables to represent the pronunciation of all words with initial /h/. In the data set there are 821 examples of word forms beginning with /h/. The twelve variables specify sounds beginning with the front of the word and moving towards the end of the word. As a result, all one and two syllable word forms that differ in pronunciation are in fact distinguished by these twelve variables. The only overlapping of word forms occurs with related words that are too long for the twelve variables to specify the difference (which occurs at the end of the words). In all there are sixty-six overlapping word forms in the total data set. Typical examples include the following:

habitual / habitually
hamburger / hamburgers
Harris's / Harrison
humanism / humanistic
hypotheses / hypothesis / hypothesized

Another general principle used in selecting the variables is the principle of proximity: we select those variables that are closest to the variable whose outcome we are trying to predict. For example, when trying to predict the spelling of the initial /h/, we do not specify the third vowel in a word as a variable without also specifying the first two vowels in the word (since these vowels are closer to the initial /h/). This principle of proximity favors local predictability. As a result it will be more difficult to account for behavior that is affected by more distant variables.

In specifying the pronunciation, I have restricted my representations to variables that directly represent phonemes and syllable structure. I have purposely avoided using distinctive features to represent phonological similarity. This decision prevents an extraordinary increase in the number of variables. But another important reason for not using distinctive feature representation is that features, when treated as *independent* variables, clearly make false predictions about phonetic similarity. Consider as an example the phonetic similarity between *beet* /bit/ and the following two words: *bought* /bɔt/ and *mid* /mɪd/. Each of these words differs from *beet* in three distinctive features:

> *bought* /bɔt/ versus *beet* /bit/:
>
> > /ɔ/ is a round, low, back vowel
> > /i/ is an unround, high, front vowel
>
> *mid* /mɪd/ versus *beet* /bit/:
>
> > /m/ is nasal, /b/ is non-nasal
> > /ɪ/ is short (or "lax"), /i/ is long (or "tense")
> > /d/ is voiced, /t/ is voiceless

Yet quite clearly *beet* and *bought* are perceived as phonetically close, while *beet* and *mid* are not at all. If we treat distinctive features as independent variables, we incorrectly predict an equality of phonetic similarity. By using only phonemic identity, we get much better results: there is only one phonemic difference between *beet* and *bought,* but three between *beet* and *mid.* Ultimately, we will need to build in some use of distinctive features (since *bit* is phonetically closer to *beet* than *bought* is), but the distinctive features cannot be independent variables.[1] So for the purposes of this book (as a book on analogical models of language and not phonological theory),

---

[1] For experimental support for these observations, see Derwing and Nearey 1986:204.

I have decided to ignore distinctive features and rely on only phonemic and syllabic variables for measuring phonological similarity.

Finally, having outlined the principles that determine the selection of variables, let us consider the question of whether the occurrences in the data set should represent tokens or types of occurrence. In principle, the representation should be based on tokens, but computer limitations sometimes require the use of types. For instance, in this book there are two large data sets (the spelling of initial /h/ in English and the past tense form in Finnish). Ultimately, the occurrences in these two data sets should directly reflect the frequency of occurrence for each word type, but given the limitations on the size of the data set, this was not possible. In all the other cases (with the exception of the somewhat artificial voicing example in this chapter) I have constructed the data set to reflect actual frequencies of occurrence. Ultimately, the difference between type and token can be eliminated by specifying enough variables. By increasing the number of variables every token occurrence will also represent a single type.

2. Categorical Behavior: The Indefinite Article

IN a rule approach, the description of the indefinite article is very simple:

> if the next word begins with a consonant,
> the indefinite article is *a* (as in *a boy*);
>
> if the next word begins with a vowel,
> the indefinite article is *an* (as in *an apple*).

Using an analogical approach, we find the solution is not so easy, yet the same basic results are obtained. In order to predict the behavior of the indefinite article, I first constructed the data set by taking all the examples of the indefinite article from a paper I wrote in 1985 entitled "Through a Glass Darkly" (published, with some changes, as Skousen 1986). In this paper there are 164 occurrences of the indefinite article, of which 136 (or 82.9%) are *a,* which compares with 86.1% *a* (23,071 out of a total of 26,810) in the Brown corpus (Francis and Kučera 1982). In order to predict the indefinite article, I selected the following nine variables:

1,3	the syllabic category (Consonant or Vowel) of the two immediately preceding phonemes
2,4	the two immediately preceding phonemes
5	whether the indefinite article begins an independent phrase (|) or not (+)
6,8	the syllabic category of the two immediately following phonemes
7,9	the two immediately following phonemes

A few sample analyses follow:

ACTUAL TEXT	OUTCOME	VARIABLES
through a glass darkly	*a*	CrVu+CgCl
played an important part	*an*	VeiCd+VɪCm
as a first example	*a*	VæCz+CfVɚ
night – an inn	*an*	VaiCt|VɪCn
to an example	*an*	CtVu+VɛCg
for a house	*a*	VɔCr+ChVau
as a youth	*a*	VæCz+CyVu
to a human messenger	*a*	CtVu+ChCy
behold, a woman	*a*	ClCd|CwVʊ

The pronunciations are essentially my own, but restricted to those found in the standard collegiate dictionaries.[2]

---

[2] For a list of the computer representations for the phonemes of English, see appendix 1. In appendix 2.1 there is a complete list of the 164 occurrences of *a/an* for this data set.

Now consider some predictions based on this data base of only 164 occurrences, where an asterisk (*) indicates that the given context occurs in the data set:

GIVEN CONTEXT	SPECIFICATION	PREDICTION (%)	
		a	*an*
picked _ apple	CkCt+VæCp	0.8	99.2
picked _ orange	CkCt+VɔCr	0.8	99.2
picked _ pear	CkCt+CpVɛ	100	0
upon _ time	VɑCn+CtVai	100	0
* *at _ gnat*	VæCt+CnVæ	100	0
say. _ honest	CsVei|VɑCn	1.1	98.9
pay. _ university	CpVei|CyVu	100	0
he's _ Hawaiian[3]	ViCz+VəCw	1.0	99.0

In these examples, there is some slight leakage of *an* → *a* (about one percent of the time), but none for *a* → *an*. Of course, this observation is from the viewpoint of a rule approach. In an analogical approach, we would simply say that vowel-initial words following the indefinite article have a small chance of taking *a,* but consonant-initial words have virtually no chance of taking *an.* The predicted results look almost rule governed, but in actual fact there are no rules.

An Acquisitional Point of View

EVEN when the number of occurrences is small, there is a strong tendency to replace *an* by *a,* but hardly any chances of the opposite occurring. In this section we make predictions for an increasing data base, beginning with only the first occurrence and adding the occurrences one at a time until we

---

[3] In my speech the initial /h/ in *Hawaiian* is not pronounced when this word is preceded by the indefinite article. In other words, when predicting the indefinite article, *Hawaiian* will be considered vowel initial.

get the expected *an* outcome at a permanent level of less than two percent of leakage. In the following scatter plot of our four vowel-initial examples, we see how the predicted probability of the outcome *an* approaches one as the data increases:

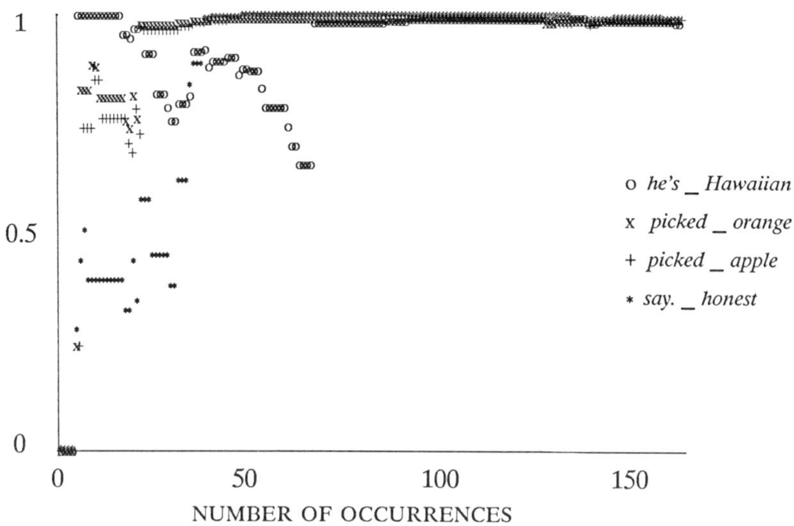

For our four other given contexts (*picked* _ *pear, upon* _ *time, at* _ *gnat, pay.* _ *university*), the word following the indefinite article begins with a consonant. And for our given sequence of occurrences, the analogical approach predicts the outcome *a* at 100.0% for every occurrence, although a minor case of leakage for *picked* _ *pear* is found from the twenty-second through the thirtieth occurrence, with the probability of *an* ranging from 1/2105 to 1/3953 (that is, from 0.000496 to 0.000253).

This analysis assumes that the speaker knows that both outcomes *a* and *an* are possible. In the initial stages of acquisition, we may reasonably assume that the speaker will first learn the more frequent outcome, *a*. At such a stage, only the outcome *a* could be predicted. But once the speaker learns that *an* is also a possible outcome, then the chances of *an* being predicted (when the following word is vowel initial) will steadily increase as the number of occurrences in the data base increases. Moreover, not every vowel-initial word will "learn" the *an* outcome in the same way, as we can see from the scatter plot of our four vowel-initial examples. Even so, each vowel-initial word will eventually predict the *an* outcome at a minimal level of leakage. For our four examples of vowel-initial words a residual level of no more than two percent leakage is reached between thirty-two and sixty-eight data occurrences. In contrast to *an,* there would be little tendency at any time for the speaker to incorrectly replace outcome *a* with *an.* This dissymmetry in behavior is due to the fact that throughout the overall contextual space the *a* outcome is more densely distributed than *an* is.

Crucial Data Missing

SUPPOSE the indefinite article plus the following segment (the crucial information for the rule approach) is blocked out by noise or silence. In other words, there is an initial sound, but the speaker has no idea what sound it is. Nonetheless, using an analogical approach, we can still predict the indefinite article. In this example we will only use information about the following sounds to predict the indefinite article. We first find the next five phonemes (within the same word) that follow the article. For these five phonemes we also determine their syllabic representations (as consonants or vowels). In all we have ten variables. If the word following the indefinite article does not contain five phonemes, we place a zero (ø) after the last phoneme and follow the zero by a string composed of the non-specification symbol, the equals sign (=). Here are a few examples:

ACTUAL TEXT	OUTCOME	VARIABLES
through a glass darkly	*a*	CgClVæCsø=
played an important part	*an*	VɪCmCpVɔCr
as a first example	*a*	CfVɚCrCsCt
night – an inn	*an*	VɪCnø=====
to an example	*an*	VɛCgCzVæCm
for a house	*a*	ChVauCsø===
as a youth	*a*	CyVuCθø===
to a human messenger	*a*	ChCyVuCmVə
behold, a woman	*a*	CwVʊCmVəCn

In most cases, the correct prediction is made even when the crucial variable is missing! We make these predictions by ignoring the first two variables in the given context (that is, by setting these two variables equal to the non-specification symbol). As before, items marked with an asterisk (*) are actual occurrences in the data set, and the probability (*Pr*) of outcome *a* occurring is given in percent:

EXAMPLE	SPECIFICATION	*Pr*(*a*)	SIGNIFICANT ANALOGIES
* *a great*	==CrVeiCtø=	100	*great* (21.1%)
* *an inn*	==Cnø=====	0	*inn* (14.5%)
a nice	==VaiCsø===	100	—
* *a gnat*	==VæCtø===	100	—
* *an evil*	==CvVəClø=	0	*evil* (40.4%)
an apple	==CpVəClø=	0	*evil, open* (27.5% each)
a crummy	==CrVəCmVi	63.2	*grammar* (11.7%)
a grin	==CrVɪCnø=	96.4	*printing* (17.9%)
an errant	==CrVəCnCt	85.3	*printing* (21.1%)

The reason for this high degree of predictability is two-fold. Sometimes the influence of particular words can be quite high, especially when the given occurs in the data. For instance, in the first example, the word *great* accounts for 21.1% of the analogical set. In such cases, word recognition plays a significant role in predicting *a*/*an*.

In other cases, *a*/*an* is predicted in terms of redundancy. For instance, in the second example, *an* is predicted because in the data /n/ is always preceded by a vowel, never a consonant (*institute, inn, increase, interesting, inner, incorrect, inspired, introduction*). In the third example, *a* is predicted because in the data a non-initial vowel is always preceded by a consonant; there are no word-initial sequences of two vowels in the data.

In the last three examples, we get a mixture of redundancy and word recognition. If the second phoneme is /r/, it can be immediately preceded by a vowel or by a consonant, but in the data there are more cases of /r/ being immediately preceded by a consonant (such as /g/, /k/, or /p/).

3. Exceptional/Regular Behavior: Spelling Initial /h/

IN this section we will show how an analogical approach predicts the spelling of the initial /h/ phoneme in English orthography. The regular outcome is, of course, the <h> grapheme. Our list of words is composed of those word forms in the Brown corpus (Francis and Kučera 1982) that have an initial /h/ phoneme and occurred in at least two different samples. Of the 821 items in the list, nearly all the words take the <h> spelling; a few take the spelling <wh>, while only one takes the Spanish spelling <j>:

OUTCOME	NUMBER OF ITEMS	EXAMPLES
<h>	806	*haberdashery ... hysterical*
<wh>	14	*who whole whooping whore*
<j>	1	*José*

On the basis of this list we use our analogical method to predict the spelling of the initial /h/ phoneme. Our predictions will be based solely upon the pronunciation of the given. We use the following twelve variables to represent the phonemic representation up through the third vowel of each word form in the data. Since all the words in our list begin with /h/, we do not specify the initial phoneme since it won't make any difference in the analogical prediction.

1 the stress pattern of the word: does the first stressed vowel occur in the first (1) or second (2) syllable?

2 the phoneme immediately preceding the first vowel (either /h/ as in *he* or /y/ as in *huge*)

3 the first vowel phoneme

4,5 the two phonemes that immediately follow the first vowel

6,7 the two phonemes that immediately precede the second vowel (or if there is no second vowel, then the last two phonemes in the word)

8 the second vowel phoneme (or if there is no second vowel, then this variable is ø)

9,10 the two phonemes that immediately follow the second vowel

11 the phoneme that immediately precedes the third vowel or, if there is no third vowel but there is a second one, then the last phoneme in the word

12 the third vowel phoneme (or if there is no third vowel but there is a second one, then this variable is ø)

In all other cases, whenever a variable cannot be assigned a phoneme or ø, that variable is marked with the non-specification symbol (=).

Some sample representations are:[4]

WORD	OUTCOME	VARIABLES
he	h	1hi==hiø====
his	h	1hɪz=ɪzø====
her	h	1hɚr=ɚrø====
who	wh	1hu==huø====
him	h	1hɪm=ɪmø====
himself	h	1hɪmsmsɛlffø
however	h	1hauɛvhauɛvɚvɚ
human	h	1yumɘumɘn=nø
hundred	h	1hɘnddrɘd=dø
hotel	h	2houtɛoutɛl=lø
Henrietta	h	1hɛnrnriɛtiɛ
Hebrew	h	1hibrbru==uø
heartbreaking	h	1hɑrtbreikɪkɪ
José	j	2houzeiouzei==eiø

[4] For a complete list of the words and their phonemic analysis, see appendix 2.2. Also see appendix 1, which converts the computer representations found in appendix 2.2 into standard phonemic representations.

We first apply our analogical approach to some words that are not in our list. In nearly all cases only the regular <h> spelling is predicted, with no leakage at all towards the irregular <wh> and <j> spellings:

WORD	PRONUNCIATION	SPECIFICATION
haddock	hæ^{1}dək	1hædəædək=kø
hafnium	hæ^{1}fniəm	1hæfnfniəmiə
halibut	hæ^{1}ləbət	1hæləæləbəbə
hallelujah	hæ$_2$ləlu^{1}yə	1hæləæləlulu
hallucination	həlu$_2$sənei^{1}šən	2həluəlusəsə
hammock	hæ^{1}mək	1hæməæmək=kø
Hanukkah	hɑ^{1}nəkə	1hɑnəɑnəkəkə
harpoon	hɑrpu^{1}n	2hɑrprpun=nø
hash	hæš	1hæš=æšø====
hassle	hæ^{1}səl	1hæsəæsəl=lø
haversack	hæ^{1}vɚrsæ$_2$k	1hævɚævɚrssæ
hearken	hɑ^{1}rkən	1hɑrkrkən=nø
hearse	hɚrs	1hɚrsrsø====
heath	hiθ	1hiθ=iθø====
helicopter	hɛ^{1}ləkɑ$_2$ptɚr	1hɛləɛləkɑkɑ
hemlock	hɛ^{1}mlɑ$_2$k	1hɛmlmlɑk=kø
hemoglobin	hi^{1}məglou$_2$bən	1himəiməgllou
hepatitis	hɛ$_2$pətai^{1}təs	1hɛpəɛpətaitai
heptagon	hɛ^{1}ptəgɑ$_2$n	1hɛptptəgɑgɑ
hermit	hɚ^{1}rmət	1hɚrmrmət=tø
heron	hɛ^{1}rən	1hɛrəɛrən=nø
hew	hyu	1yu==yuø====
hibernate	hai^{1}bɚrnei$_2$t	1haibɚaibɚrnnei
hiccup	hɪ^{1}kəp	1hɪkəɪkəp=pø
hieroglyphic	hai$_2$rəglɪ^{1}fɪk	1hairəairəgllɪ
hippie	hɪ^{1}pi	1hɪpiɪpi==iø
hippopotamus	hɪ$_2$pəpɑ^{1}təməs	1hɪpəɪpəpɑpɑ
hockey	hɑ^{1}ki	1hɑkiɑki==iø
hominy	hɑ^{1}məni	1hɑməɑmənini
homonym	hɑ^{1}mənɪ$_2$m	1hɑməɑmənɪnɪ

hornet	hɔ^{1}rnət	1hɔrnrnət=tø
hubbub	hə^{1}bə$_2$b	1həbəəbəb=bø
hullabaloo	hə^{1}ləbəlu$_2$	1hələələbəbə
humbug	hə^{1}mbə$_2$g	1həmbmbəg=gø
humdinger	hə^{1}mdɪ^{1}ŋɚr	1həmdmdɪŋɚŋɚ
humdrum	hə^{1}mdrə$_2$m	1həmddrəm=mø
hump	həmp	1həmpmpø====
humus	hyu^{1}məs	1yuməuməs=sø
hutch	həč	1həč=əčø====
hyacinth	hai^{1}əsɪ$_2$nθ	1haiəshaiəsɪsɪ
hybrid	hai^{1}brəd	1haibrbrəd=dø
hydrant	hai^{1}drənt	1haidrdrənttø
hydraulic	haidrɔ^{1}lɪk	2haidrdrɔlɪlɪ
hyena	haii^{1}nə	2haiinhaiinənə
hypnotize	hɪ^{1}pnətai$_2$z	1hɪpnpnətaitai
hypotenuse	haipɑ^{1}tənu$_2$s	2haipɑaipɑtətə

In a few cases there is some minor leakage towards the <wh> spelling:

WORD	PRONUNCIATION	PROBABILITY (IN PERCENT) OF OUTCOME <wh>
hacienda	hɑ$_2$siɛ^{1}ndə	0.06
hoe	hou	7.42
hone	houn	0.09

For each of these examples we can determine the number of pointers in the analogical set that take the exceptional <wh> spelling:

WORD	GIVEN CONTEXT	TOTAL NUMBER OF POINTERS	ANALOGICAL SOURCES FOR OUTCOME <wh>
hacienda	1hɑsiɑsiɛniɛ	56124	*whosoever* 36
hoe	1hou==houø====	1011	*whole* 48, *who* 27
hone	1houn=ounø====	26420	*whole* 24

There are also a couple examples of minor leakage towards the exceptional <j> spelling:

WORD	PRONUNCIATION	PROBABILITY (IN PERCENT) OF OUTCOME <j>
hooray	hʊrei^{1}	0.11
hosanna	houzæ^{1}nə	0.04

Of course, in these examples the exceptional behavior comes from a single word, *José:*

WORD	GIVEN CONTEXT	TOTAL NUMBER OF POINTERS	ANALOGICAL SOURCES FOR OUTCOME <j>
hooray	2hʊreiʊrei==eiø	19279	*José* 22
hosanna	2houzæouzænənə	55380	*José* 24

These two words differ from *José* in only four variables. (We ignore the non-specified ninth and tenth variables in {2houzeiouzei==eiø}.)

We now consider the effect of exceptional words on the surrounding contextual space. We list a number of words at increasing distances from the exceptional *José*. For each word, we determine the number of variables that disagree with the specification of *José*. We refer to this difference in variable specification as the distance from *José*. All the words at a distance of five or greater are of Spanish origin and were taken from Merriam Webster's *Ninth New Collegiate Dictionary,* 1983 edition. These words are assigned an English rather than a Spanish pronunciation. The three items marked with an asterisk (*) have been given artificial pronunciations in order to construct examples closer to *José*. As before, the probability is given in percent. In general, the closer a word is to *José* the greater the chances of that word taking the <j> spelling. In fact, the relationship appears to be exponential:

	WORD	PRONUNCIATION	SPECIFICATION	PROBABILITY OF OUTCOME <h>	<wh>	<j>
0	*José*	houzei^1	2houzeiouzei==eiø	-	-	100
1	**Josef*	houzei^{1}f	2houzeiouzeif=fø	35.9	-	64.1
2	**José*	housei^1	2houseiousei==eiø	85.9	0.9	13.2
3	**Josef*	houzɛ^{1}f	2houzɛouzɛf=fø	96.8	-	3.2
4	*hooray*	hʊrei^1	2hʊreiʊrei==eiø	99.9	-	0.1
	hosanna	houzæ^{1}nə	2houzæouzænənə	100.0	-	0.0
5	*Jolo*	houlou^1	2houlououlou==ouø	99.5	-	0.5
	Jerez	hərei^{1}s	2həreiəreis=sø	100.0	-	0.0
6	*Jiménez*	himei^{1}nəs	2himeiimeinənə	100.0	-	0.0
	Jaén	hɑei^{1}n	2hɑeinhɑein=nø	100.0	-	0.0
7	*Jujuy*	huhwi^1	2huhwiuhwi==iø	99.9	0.0	0.1
	Junín	huni^{1}n	2huniunin=nø	100.0	0.0	0.0
	jacal	həkɑ^{1}l	2həkɑəkɑl=lø	100	-	-
8	*Jalisco*	həlɪ^{1}skou	2həlɪəlɪskkou	100.0	0.0	-
	Jalapa	həlɑ^{1}pə	2həlɑəlɑpəpə	100	-	-
	Júcar	hu^{1}kɑ$_2$r	1hukɑukɑr=rø	100	-	-
	jai alai	hai^{1}lai$_2$	1hailaiailai==aiø	100	-	-
	jojoba	həhou^{1}bə	2həhouəhoubəbə	100	-	-
9	*jipijapa*	hi$_2$pihɑ^{1}pə	1hipiipihɑhɑ	100	-	-

Measuring Exceptionality

THERE are two ways of looking at the exceptionality of the spellings <wh> and <j>. Essentially, both views reflect the fact that these two spellings are isolated in the contextual space; that is, they are surrounded by regular behavior. On the other hand, nearly every occurrence of the regular spelling, <h>, is surrounded by regular behavior.

(1) Excluding the Given Context from the Data Set:

Suppose that the given context occurs in the data, but that its listed behavior is ignored when we determine the analogical set – that is, we act as if the given context is excluded from the data set. If the surrounding occurrences behave like the given context, then the predicted behavior will remain the same. In such a case, we say that the listed behavior of the given is *regular.* On the other hand, if surrounding occurrences behave differently from the given context, then the predicted behavior of the given context will change. In such a case, the listed behavior of the given will be considered *exceptional.* In applying this approach to our data, we find that every word spelled with initial <wh> or <j> is exceptional:

WORD	SPECIFICATION	PROBABILITY (%) OF OUTCOME		
		<h>	<wh>	<j>
who	1hu==huø====	80.8	19.2	-
whom	1hum=umø====	99.9	0.1	-
whose, who's	1huz=uzø====	99.8	0.2	-
whoever	1huɛvhuɛvɚvɚ	99.8	0.2	-
who'd	1hud=udø====	99.9	0.1	-
whosoever	1husouusouɛvouɛ	99.3	0.7	-
whole	1houl=oulø====	100	-	-
wholly	1houllli==iø	98.8	1.2	-
wholesome	1houlslsəm=mø	100.0	0.0	-
wholesale	1houlslseil=lø	99.8	0.2	-
wholly-owned	1houllliouniou	51.6	48.4	-
whore	1hɔr=ɔrø====	100	-	-
whooping	1hupɪupɪŋ=ŋø	100	-	-
José	2houzeiouzei==eiø	99.9	0.1	-

In two cases only do we get some strong probability of the exceptional <wh> spelling. The given *who* is strongly supported by its related forms *whose, whom, who's, whoever,* and *who'd.* And the reason for the nearly split behavior of *wholly-owned* is due to the base word *wholly.* If in our analysis we exclude all morphologically related forms as well as the given context, then the regular <h> spelling would be overwhelmingly predicted for *who* and *wholly-owned.* Note that in this data set there are no morphologically related forms for the three words *whore, whooping,* and *José.* And when these words are excluded, the regular <h> spelling is highly favored. In fact, in the case of *whore* and *whooping,* there is no leakage at all towards the exceptional spellings.

When this same approach is applied to words spelled with <h>, the regular <h> spelling is again predicted:

WORD	SPECIFICATION	PROBABILITY (%) OF OUTCOME		
		<h>	<wh>	<j>
he	1hi==hiø====	99.2	0.8	-
his	1hɪz=ɪzø====	99.9	0.1	-
hand	1hændndø====	100	-	-
human	1yuməumən=nø	100	-	-
hands	1hænddzø====	100	-	-
hotel	2houtɛoutɛl=lø	100.0	0.0	-
happy	1hæpiæpi==iø	100	-	-
hole	1houl=oulø====	100	-	-

(2) Measuring the Gang Effect:

We can also consider what happens when the given context occurs in the data and is not excluded. In such a case the predicted behavior of the given context will be determined by its actual behavior in the data set. The analogical set will contain occurrences of the given context, but it may also contain other occurrences that behave like the given context. In such a case, the behavior of the given context is supported by these other occurrences. For instance, when we use *he* (that is, {1hi==hiø===–}) as the given context and we do not exclude *he* from the data, we find that the analogical set not only contains *he,* but many other words besides. In fact, of the 3128 pointers in the analogical set for *he,* only 192 point to *he;* the rest (2936) point to words other than *he.* Thus only 6.1% of the analogical set for *he* is due to *he* itself.

We can give an explicit formula to measure this gang effect.[5] We desire the following properties in our measure: (1) if there is no gang effect (that is, all the pointers in the analogical set point to the given context), then the measure equals zero; (2) if the number of pointers in the analogical set pointing to the given context is halved (thus leading to an increase in the gang effect), then the measure increases by one. These two properties lead to a logarithmic measure of the gang effect. If we let f represent the fraction of the analogical set that points to the given context (that is, f is the analogical effect of the given context), then the gang effect for the given context is defined as follows:

$$\text{gang effect (given context)} = -\log_2 f$$

In other words, we first determine the analogical effect of the given context. We then calculate the gang effect by taking the negative logarithm (to the base two) of this analogical effect. In the example of *he* the fraction f is 192/3128. Thus the gang effect for *he* is the negative logarithm of this fraction:

$$\text{gang effect } (\textit{he}) = -\log_2(192/3128) = -\log_2 0.06138 = 4.026$$

Regularly behaving occurrences tend to have rather high gang effects. On the other hand, exceptionally behaving occurrences have low gang effects, ones that are near zero. Consider, for instance, the analogical set for *José*. When *José* is the given context (that is, {2houzeiouzei==eiø}) and *José* is not excluded from the data set, then the predicted spelling is <j> and all 906 pointers in the analogical set for *José* point to only *José*. Under these conditions, the gang effect will be zero:

$$\text{gang effect } (\textit{José}) = -\log_2(906/906) = -\log_2 1 = 0$$

Applying this measure of the gang effect to our previous examples we get low values (all under one) for the exceptional occurrences in the data, but generally high values (normally greater than three) for the regular

---

[5] I owe this term "gang effect" to McClelland and Rumelhart 1980, part I:59-64, although they use the term with respect to a connectionist rather than an analogical approach. See section 4.2 for a comparison of these two approaches.

occurrences. In the following list, we give once more the probability of getting a non-<h> outcome when the given context is excluded from the data. In those cases where there is at least one percent leakage in favor of the non-<h> outcomes, the gang effect is always greater than zero, but less than one. Those items with at least one percent leakage are marked with an asterisk (*).

WORD	GANG EFFECT	PROBABILITY (%) OF LEAKAGE
exceptional		
**who*	0.737	19.2
whom	0	0.1
whose, who's	0	0.2
whoever	0.015	0.2
who'd	0	0.1
whosoever	0	0.7
**wholly*	0.734	1.2
wholesome	0.120	0.0
wholesale	0.115	0.2
**wholly-owned*	0.170	48.4
whore	0	0
whooping	0	0
José	0	0.1
regular		
he	4.026	0.8
his	5.383	0.1
hand	5.495	0
human	4.216	0
hands	5.721	0
hotel	3.337	0.0
happy	5.005	0
homophones		
whole, hole	0	0

Of particular interest is the result for the homophone pair *whole* and *hole*. Both these words have the same pronunciation – and thus the same variable specification, {1houl=oulø====}. Depending on which of these words are included in the data, we get different values for the gang effect as well as the probability of the exceptional spelling <wh>:

WORDS INCLUDED IN THE DATA	GANG EFFECT	PROBABILITY (%) OF OUTCOME <wh>
both *whole* and *hole*	0	50.0
only *whole*	0	100
only *hole*	4.218	0
neither one	not defined	0

In other words, when *whole* is included in the data, the gang effect for both *whole* and *hole* is reduced to zero. The only possibility for *hole* to have a non-zero gang effect occurs when *whole* is excluded.

Overall, these results mean that in Modern English the only time the exceptional spelling <wh> will occur as a *common* spelling error for initial /h/ is in cases of homophony. Thus, we readily expect mixups of *whoop* and *hoop, wholly* and *holy,* and *whore* and *hoar(frost)* as well as *whole* and *hole.* But other extensions of <wh> should be relatively infrequent. Although there are a number of <wh> words, they do not work together to form a significant gang effect of their own.

We should note that all the <wh> words have an <o> spelling, which means that originally in Middle English these words all had a similar vowel pronunciation – namely, a mid back rounded vowel. In Middle English these words probably formed a minor gang effect. The <wh> spelling for initial /h/ comes from a consonant cluster simplification: when immediately preceded by a consonant and immediately followed by a mid round vowel, /w/ was deleted in late Middle English (thus *two* /twō/ > /tō/, *sword* /sword/ > /sord/, and *who* /hwō/ > /hō/). Originally, the frequently occurring *who* and its related forms (*whom, whose,* and so on) served as the source for the <wh> spelling of /h/. Before the stabilization of spelling, this exceptional spelling served as the analogical source for the spelling of other words that began with /h/ followed by a mid round vowel. Thus from the fifteenth to seventeenth centuries, the <wh> spelling was not only extended to *whole, whore,* and *whoop,* but there were also spellings such as WHOM for *home,* WHOTE for *hot,* WHOOD for *hood,* and WHOORD for *hoard* (Scragg 1974:59). But in Modern English this tendency to extend the <wh> spelling no longer exists. In part this may be due to the standardization of spelling, but we should note that an analogical analysis also predicts the virtual exceptionality of the <wh> spelling in Modern English. The reason for this is that later changes in pronunciation have served to weaken the minor gang effect that this exceptional <wh> spelling would have had in Middle English. The so-called Great Vowel Shift, for instance, raised the long mid vowels of *who* and *whoop* to /ū/, but the mid vowels of *whole* and *whore* stayed as mid vowels, thus weakening the original gang effect for the <wh> spelling.

4. Idiosyncratic Behavior: Voicing Onset Time

IN this example we apply our analogical approach to the problem of voicing onset time (VOT). In section 1.2 we referred to the perceptual tests that Lisker and Abramson have carried out which show a region of shifting towards the voiceless stops as voicing onset time is increased. In order to model the transitional behavior between voiced and voiceless stops in English, we need to construct a data set that represents two types of voicing in English. Some speakers (such as myself) produce voiced stops with prevoicing; other speakers produce voiced stops with voicing onset occurring simultaneously (or nearly so) with release of the stop.[6]

I constructed the data set for this example in the following way. I first collected twenty tokens of word-initial labial stops from my own pronunciation of single words, ten of /b/ and ten of /p/. (The words were pronounced from a list, with some pause between each word.) I then measured the VOT for each of these tokens, with the following resulting distribution of voicing onset times (in milliseconds):

b	-107	-97	-83	-71	-58	-53	-49	-48	-32	-19
p	51	63	63	70	71	73	83	83	88	94

[6] For further discussion of this division in the population, see Lisker and Abramson 1964:394-395.

I then included in the data set an additional twenty hypothetical tokens to represent the other kind of speaker: ten tokens of the voiced stop /b/ with +0 to +2 msec of VOT, plus a repetition of the ten tokens of the voiceless stop /p/:

b	0	0	0	1	1	1	1	2	2	2
p	51	63	63	70	71	73	83	83	88	94

There appears to be very little variation in VOT for speakers that produce the non-prevoiced /b/. For instance, in Lisker and Abramson 1964:394 we find a range of only +0 to +5 msec for fifty-one tokens of non-prevoiced /b/ (and an average of +1 msec). Similarly, in Lisker and Abramson 1970:566 we find that for the interval of measurement (five milliseconds) there is no variance at all for the non-prevoiced /b/; all the examples are assigned a VOT of +0 msec, so that we may presume that the actual measurements were all within the interval [-2.5,2.5]. Because of these measurements the ten tokens of non-prevoiced /b/ are restricted to the interval [0,2].

Unlike the case of /b/, the two studies by Lisker and Abramson (1964 and 1970) do not suggest any division in population for the VOT of the voiceless stop /p/. I therefore derived the ten additional tokens of the voiceless stop by simply repeating the ten tokens from my own pronunciation of /p/.

From these VOT values, I then constructed the data set by assigning seven variables between +2 (the maximal VOT for /b/) and +51 (the minimal VOT for /p/):

VARIABLE	INTERVAL OF TIME
1	(-1.5, 5.5]
2	(5.5, 12.5]
3	(12.5, 19.5]
4	(19.5, 26.5]
5	(26.5, 33.5]
6	(33.5, 40.5]
7	(40.5, 47.5]

For each of the forty VOT values I determined which of these seven intervals contained voicing. If any voicing occurred in an interval, I marked that variable with an *x*, otherwise with an *o*. In this way the continuous variable of voicing between +2 and +51 msec was assigned a discrete sequence of *o*'s and *x*'s. The resulting variable analysis was *xxxxxxx* for each occurrence of /b/ and *ooooooo* for each /p/, as in the following examples:[7]

VOT	OUTCOME	VARIABLE ANALYSIS
-107	*b*	*xxxxxxx*
-19	*b*	*xxxxxxx*
0	*b*	*xxxxxxx*
2	*b*	*xxxxxxx*
51	*p*	*ooooooo*
51	*p*	*ooooooo*
94	*p*	*ooooooo*
94	*p*	*ooooooo*

Using this data, we can analogically predict the probability of /b/ or /p/ for various VOTs, including ones which are, in some sense, "deviant" or "impossible" – namely, the ones between /b/ and /p/:

VOT	VARIABLE ANALYSIS	PROBABILITY (%) OF OUTCOME /b/
-1.5	*xxxxxxx*	100
5.5	*oxxxxxx*	98.4
12.5	*ooxxxxx*	91.2
19.5	*oooxxxx*	68.2
26.5	*ooooxxx*	31.8
33.5	*oooooxx*	8.8
40.5	*ooooooх*	1.6
47.5	*ooooooo*	0

[7] For a complete list of the data and its analysis, see appendix 2.3.

In the following graph, we represent these predicted results with the solid line (——) and compare it with the experimental results given in Lisker and Abramson 1970:566. The experimental results are represented by the broken line (--------):

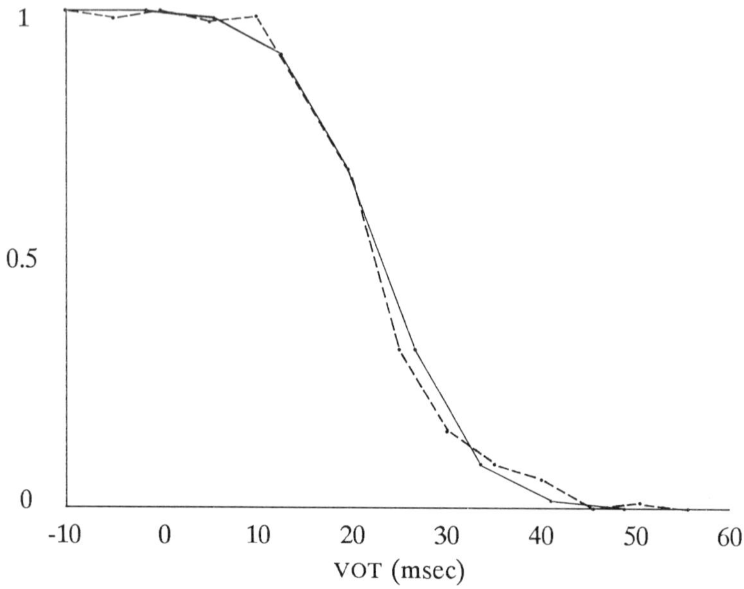

The predicted transition closely matches the results from Lisker and Abramson's perceptual experiments (1970:566), not only in slope but also in the crossover point (where the probability of /b/ and /p/ are equal), which occurs somewhere between +20 and +25 msec for /b,p/ in English.

One parameter that should be considered is the number of variables (v). If we increase the number of variables, we obtain a tighter transition from /b/ to /p/; if we decrease the number of variables, the transition becomes flatter. The best fit occurs when we select seven variables, although a fairly close fit can be obtained for five to nine variables. In the following graph we compare Lisker and Abramson's results with the analogical predictions for $v = 5$ and $v = 9$:

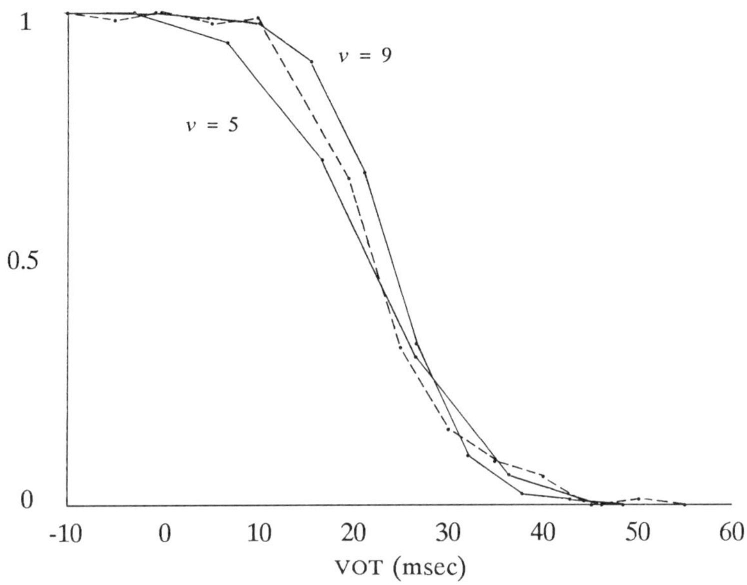

The number of variables determines the length of time assigned to each variable:

NUMBER OF VARIABLES	LENGTH OF TIME (msec)
2	24.50
3	16.33
4	12.25
5	9.80
6	8.17
7	7.00
8	6.13
9	5.44
10	4.90

The best fit of predicted and experimental results occurs when we assign a time interval between five and ten milliseconds. Interestingly, there is evidence that speakers can distinguish between sound durations differing as little as ten milliseconds – and under optimal conditions even down to two milliseconds (Lehiste 1970:10-13). The analogical predictions of /b,p/ transitions are thus in general agreement with the capacity of speakers to distinguish sound duration.

This example shows that an analogical approach can handle a continuous variable by analyzing it as a sequence of discrete variables. It also shows that an analogical approach can predict the behavior of "impossible" contexts (such as a labial stop in English with +12 msec of voicing lag). This ability of an analogical approach to account for deviance corresponds with the abundant evidence from language usage that speakers can deal with improperly formed given contexts. An important consequence of this capability is that an analogical approach eliminates the need for Chomsky's distinction between competence and performance (Chomsky 1965:3-4). This distinction arises in rule-based approaches since rules are used to account for "normalized" behavior and performance factors are left with the task of accounting for "violations" of those rules. On the other hand, in an analogical approach the strategy used to identify /b,p/ is the same irrespective of whether the given VOT is "normal" or "abnormal". There is no independent description of the data; there is only predicted behavior for given contexts. Usage is the description, and performance is competence.

Chapter Four

PREDICTING NON-DETERMINISTIC LANGUAGE VARIATION

1. Learning Probabilities

LINGUISTS have usually tried to analyze language deterministically. Cases of variation have long been recognized, but until the 1960s these cases were vaguely identified as "free variation", a term which essentially meant that the behavior was non-deterministic. Labov and other sociolinguists have discovered many complex examples of language variation and have clearly demonstrated that language variation is not at all "free", that many factors – both linguistic and social – affect the probability of a variant occurring. Moreover, the probabilistic behavior is not only found at the group level, but also in individual speakers. And no matter how many variables are considered, the probabilistic behavior cannot be reduced to deterministic explanation. For a good example of this, see Guy's discussion of final /t,d/ deletion in English for which "variation is inherent, and cannot be scrubbed out of our linguistic description by ever-finer subdivisions of the data" (Guy 1980:11).

Besides the evidence for probabilistic behavior from linguistic studies, psychological experimentation has demonstrated that humans can learn to behave probabilistically. As an example, consider an early experiment by Grant, Hake, and Hornseth in which subjects learned to predict a given outcome at the same probability that it occurred at:

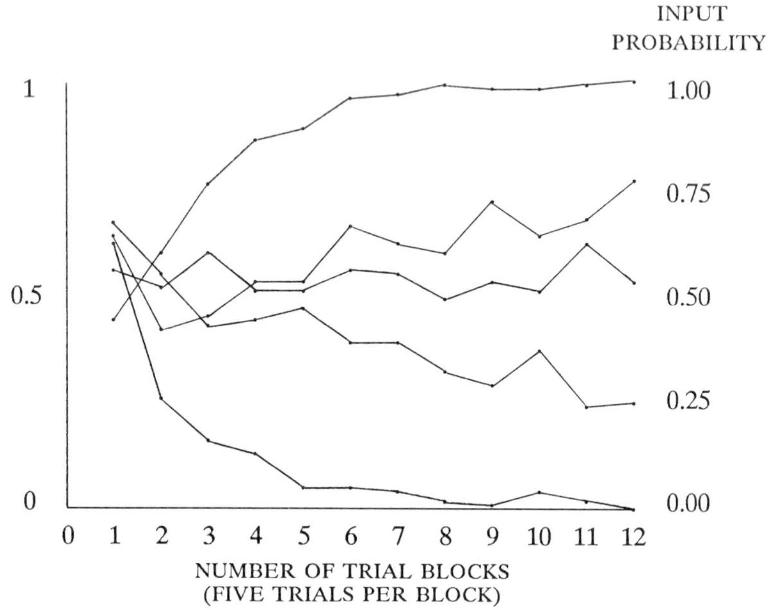

(adapted from Grant, Hake, and Hornseth 1951:2)

As far as language studies go, the question no longer is whether there is probabilistic behavior in language. Instead, the question is: How do we account for this behavior? Following the traditional assumption that language is rule governed, Labov (1970:53-57) has proposed that variable rules be used to account for probabilities. A variable rule is basically like a normal rule except that a probabilistic function is assigned to the rule. Yet there are conceptual problems with variable rules. One fundamental problem is the status of the probabilities: Do they actually exist? And if so, how are they learned from the statistics and then used to predict behavior? Many have argued that the probabilities do not in fact exist, but this still leaves us with the question of what does account for the probabilistic behavior.[1]

As an example, consider a given context that has two possible outcomes, *s* and *t*. Let us assume (for the purposes of discussion) that the probability of the *s* outcome is 1/3 and the probability of the *t* outcome is 2/3. Within a rule approach we could account for the behavior of this given context by positing a probabilistic rule:

$$Pr(s,t\,|\,\text{given context}) = (1/3,2/3)$$

One of the problems with such a rule is in its acquisition. The learner is only confronted with a sequence of *s*'s and *t*'s:

... *t s t t s t t t s s t t* ...

How then does the learner discover the probability from the statistics? Does the learner make an estimate of the probability and continually revise that estimate as additional examples of *s* and *t* occur? And having learned a probability, how does the speaker use that probability to predict the *s* outcome one third of the time?

An analogical approach avoids these problems of learning and using probabilities. In fact, by using an analogical approach we can avoid the need to predict stochastic behavior directly from probabilities. In order to show this, we will first consider how our analogical approach predicts the behavior for the simplest case, when the given context is non-empty. When the given context actually occurs, the analogical set is equivalent to the given context. To see this we first recall from section 2.2 that there are only two basic types of homogeneous contexts, (1) deterministic and (2) unobstructed non-deterministic. When the given context is deterministic, the analogical set can contain occurrences besides those found in the given context, but these additional occurrences will have the same outcome as the given context. On the other hand, when the given context is non-deterministic, the analogical set can only contain the occurrences of the given context. This

[1] See Fasold 1978 for further discussion of this problem.

is because all other occurrences, no matter what their behavior, are obstructed by the non-deterministic occurrences in the given context. In either case then, the predicted behavior of an occurring given context must be identical to the actual behavior of that context.

This means that we can predict non-deterministic behavior for non-deterministic contexts, but without directly using a probability. Suppose, for example, that the given context contains six occurrences and that two of these occurrences take the *s* outcome and four the *t* outcome:

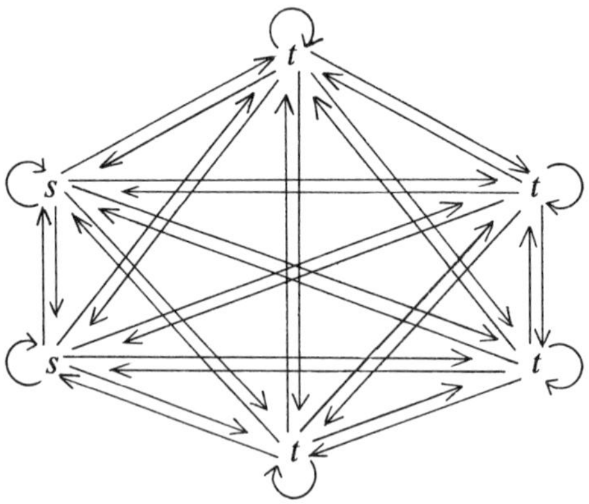

In the analogical set for this given context there will be twelve (2×6) pointers pointing to the *s* outcome and twenty-four (4×6) pointing to the *t* outcome, so that the probability of selecting the *s* outcome will be identical to its relative frequency of occurrence in the given context:

$$Pr(s\,|\,\text{given context}) = 12/(12+24) = 12/36 = 1/3$$

In general, if we have n_i occurrences of outcome i in a non-deterministic given context containing a total of n occurrences, there will be $n_i n$ pointers in the analogical set pointing to outcome i (out of a total of n^2 pointers in the analogical set). Thus the probability of predicting outcome i will be $n_i n/n^2 = n_i/n$, the relative frequency of outcome i.

Thus in an analogical approach it looks like probabilities are being learned. But in actual fact an analogical approach stores only examples. The analogical approach uses those examples to construct the analogical set (for a given context) and then randomly selects an outcome from that analogical set to predict stochastic behavior.

2. *McClelland and Rumelhart's Connectionist Approach*

ONE alternative to the analogical approach is McClelland and Rumelhart's interactive activation model (McClelland and Rumelhart 1980; Rumelhart and McClelland 1985), a connectionist model of language more recently refined and referred to as "parallel distributed processing". Such a model predicts behavior by allowing "interactions among a network of units" (Rumelhart and McClelland 1985:ii). Various possibilities compete with one another until stability is obtained. In many respects, the connectionist model is similar to the analogical one. Both approaches dispense with the need for rules, yet still account for "rule governed" behavior. They can both predict behavior when the data is ill-formed or missing crucial information. And they both allow for a "gang" effect.[2]

There is, however, one serious problem with the connectionist model of language: it does not allow direct access to the possible outcomes for a given context. This inability manifests itself in several ways. In the first place, connectionist models cannot account for the ability to learn given probabilities. Even if certain parameters are defined (see McClelland and Rumelhart 1980, part I:13-18), there is still no systematic way (except by trial and error) to set those parameters so that predicted probabilities equal actual probabilities. True, a connectionist model makes probabilistic predictions, but there is no guarantee that it can predict an outcome at the same relative frequency that the outcome actually occurs at. In other words, there is no direct way for a connectionist model to learn a probability. This is because the connectionist model does not actually define a set of occurrences to choose from. Instead, it allows the possible outcomes to compete with each other until stability is achieved.

---

[2] For more discussion on this approach, see Rumelhart, McClelland, and the PDP Research Group 1986.

Another difference between connectionist and analogical approaches deals with the possibility of alternative rules of usage. In an analogical approach, an analogical set is defined and from this set an outcome is selected. Thus far we have assumed that the outcome is selected by the rule of usage that we have referred to as *random selection:*

> *Randomly select one of the pointers in the analogical set and predict behavior according to the outcome associated with that pointer.*

But another possible rule of usage is *selection by plurality:*

> *Determine the outcome that occurs most frequently in the analogical set and predict that the given context will have the same outcome.*

Normally, there will be only one outcome that occurs most frequently. As the data increases, the probability of ties between outcomes approaches zero. Selection by plurality almost always predicts the same outcome for a given context. Even though the context itself may actually be non-deterministic in behavior, this rule of usage will almost always predict deterministic behavior for the context.

One important property of this rule of usage is that it maximizes utility. If we gain a reward every time the predicted outcome agrees with the actual outcome and if we sustain a loss (which can be thought of as a negative gain) every time our prediction is wrong, then we can maximize our overall gain by always choosing the most frequently occurring outcome.

There is substantial evidence that humans can predict behavior using either rule of usage. For instance, Messick and Solley have shown that children from ages 3-8 (like adults) can learn to predict probabilistic behavior at virtually the same relative frequency that it actually occurs at:

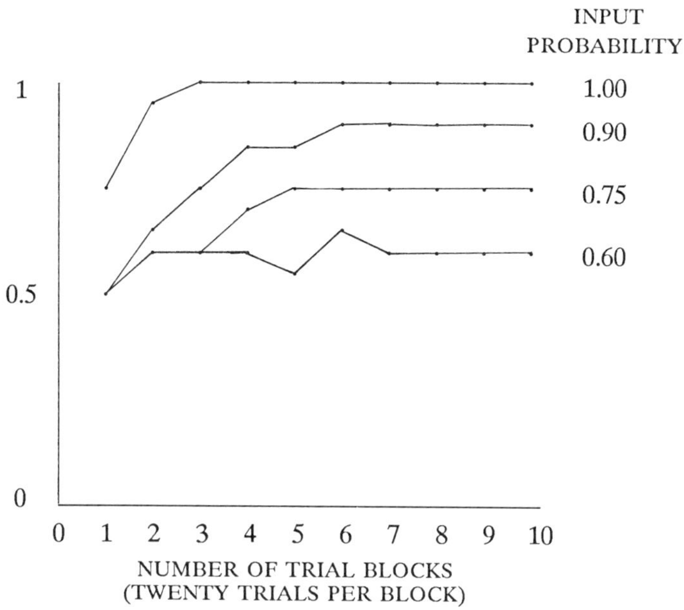

(adapted from Messick and Solley 1957:26)

But in Messick and Solley's experiments, when a reward was given to the children for correctly guessing the next outcome, the older children (ages 7-8) shifted all their guesses to the most frequent outcome. On the other hand, the youngest children (ages 3-4) continued to guess randomly and failed to use selection by plurality, the rule of usage that would have maximized their gain. Yet children as young as five years old started to use selection by plurality, but not as consistently as the older children. In the following two graphs we first see the results of Messick and Solley's non-reward experiment and then the results of their reward experiment. In both cases the input probability was 0.75.

no-reward experiment (random selection for all ages):

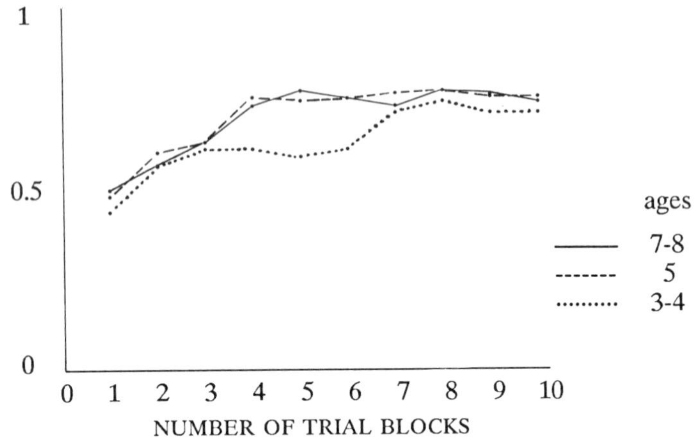

(adapted from Messick and Solley 1957:30)

reward experiment (selection by plurality for older ages):

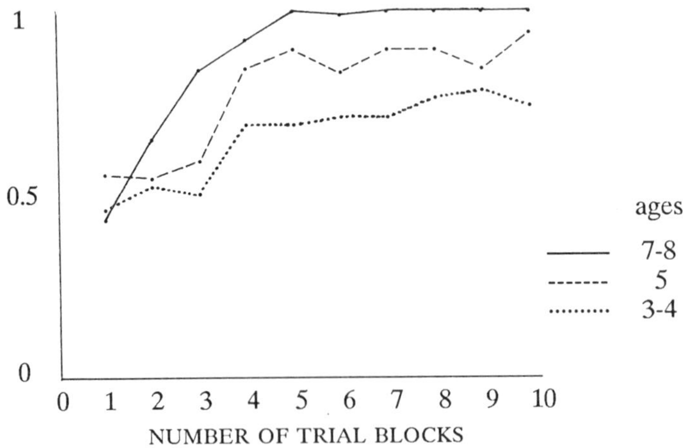

(adapted from Messick and Solley 1957:30)

This ability to switch from one rule of usage to another suggests that humans have the ability to inspect a set of possible outcomes and predict behavior according to the rule of usage they have chosen. An analogical approach makes predictions by directly selecting an outcome from the analogical set. On the other hand, the connectionist model of language does not offer such accessibility.

Speakers also have the ability to choose another outcome when additional input indicates that the original choice of outcome is wrong. For instance, when confronted with the nonce spelling YEAD, speakers typically give a pronunciation (usually /yid/) with no difficulty. In addition, when these speakers are told that their first pronunciation is incorrect and asked to produce a second pronunciation, they have no difficulty in producing an alternative (such as /yɛd/ or /yeid/). In an analogical approach we can readily extend our rules of usage to include the ability to find another outcome in the analogical set when the first outcome chosen is unacceptable. The connectionist model does not readily allow such a direct choice of alternative outcomes. In order to model this kind of ability, the connections pointing to the first outcome chosen would have to be deactivated or momentarily disconnected.

There is also evidence that speakers can alternate from one outcome to another, especially when one or more of the resulting choices may be considered strange or unacceptable by the speaker. Consider the following examples from children learning the language (taken from my own data collection):

(1) Nathaniel (5 years, 10 months):

> Looking at a picture of the Grand Canyon, N keeps trying to pronounce *cliffs:* /klɪ^{1}ftəz/, /klɪfs/, /klɪvz/, /klɪfs/.

(2) Angela (6 years, 10 months):

> The possessive form *Beth's* is pronounced first as /bɛs/ and then immediately followed by /bɛ^{1}θəz/.

A How do you add the *s* to *Beth?* It's hard to say. How do you say it?

R I say /bɛs/ [bɛs:].

A I say /bɛθ/, like *Beth house* (/bɛθ haus/).

(3) Angela (7 years, 11 months):

The plural form *ghosts* is pronounced first as /gousts/, then as /gous/, and then followed by the question "How do you pronounce that?"

3. Imperfect Memory and Multivariate Predictions

IN this section we apply the analogical approach to multivariate probabilistic data. We will consider some data from Fasold 1978:92. The data records the number of occurrences and non-occurrences of final-stop deletion in Washington, D.C., vernacular Black English in terms of three linguistic variables:

1 whether the final stop is followed by a vowel (*v*) or not (*c*);

2 whether the final stop actually ends the base word (*w*) or ends a morpheme added to the base word (*m*);

3 whether the final stop is preceded by a stop (*p*), a sonorant (*s*), or a fricative (*f*).

Using these three variables we obtain the following array of occurrences of deletion and non-deletion:

CONTEXTUAL VARIABLES			OUTCOMES		
1	2	3	deletion	non-deletion	
v	*w*	*p*	6	61	67
		s	15	48	63
		f	13	42	55
	m	*p*	12	2	14
		s	7	5	12
		f	2	3	5
c	*w*	*p*	22	13	35
		s	37	10	47
		f	24	8	32
	m	*p*	2	0	2
		s	21	4	25
		f	11	2	13
			172	198	370

We first remind ourselves that if the given context occurs the predicted behavior will be identical to the listed behavior of the given context (providing the rule of usage is random selection). When we apply the analogical approach to Fasold's data, we note, for instance, that if the given context is *vmf*, the analogical approach will predict that deletion will occur forty percent of the time (since 2×5 out of 5×5 pointers point to the deletion outcome), so that the predicted probability of deletion (40%) is equal to the relative frequency of deletion (two out of five cases). Since every possible context in Fasold's analysis actually occurs, the analogical approach (as it stands) makes no interesting predictions – that is, no predictions differ from the actual frequency of occurrence.

This preciseness in predictability is not accidental. Instead, it is related to the fact that the analogical approach is equivalent to the most powerful statistical test possible. Our statistical test rejects homogeneity under very simple conditions – whenever there is any increase in the number of disagreements (see section 2.2). This approach is equivalent to a statistical test with a level of significance of one. If any sign of potential heterogeneity occurs in a data context, then this approach decides that the context is in fact heterogeneous.

Moreover, this approach assumes that every occurrence of data is remembered, which means that each occurrence is equally important in determining heterogeneity. In fact, there is a close connection between perfect memory, precise predictability, and the most powerful statistical test possible. Correspondingly, by introducing imperfect memory into our analogical approach, we can introduce impreciseness in predictability as well as smaller, more "reasonable" levels of statistical significance.

In order to see the effects of imperfect memory on predictability, let us first consider Fasold's data independently of the three variables. In such a case, we assume that we only know the overall rate of deletion, but have no knowledge of the variables that affect the rate of deletion. (In other words, the given context is the general context --- .) In such a case, we know that there are 172 occurrences of deletion and 198 of non-deletion. Let us assume that the probability of forgetting a particular occurrence in the data set is a constant q – that is, q is the same for every occurrence in the data set and is not a function of either time or position in the data set. We further assume that this probability of forgetting a particular occurrence is independent of the probability of forgetting any other occurrence in the data set. Obviously, if $q = 0$ then we have perfect memory. If $0 < q < 1$ then we have imperfect memory. (And if $q = 1$ we have no memory at all!) As long as we remember at least one occurrence of the data, we can make some prediction about the deletion of final consonants. But if none of the occurrences are remembered, then no prediction is possible. Assuming a total of n occurrences in the data set, the probability of predictability can be readily calculated:

$$Pr(\text{prediction}) = Pr(\text{at least one occurrence remembered}) = 1 - q^n$$

$$Pr(\text{non-prediction}) = Pr(\text{no occurrences remembered}) = q^n$$

Thus the probability of non-prediction is a function of both q (the probability of forgetting an occurrence) and n (the number of occurrences in the data set). In essence, $1 - q$ (the probability of remembering an occurrence) represents the level of significance. The nearer q is to one, the greater the chances that potential heterogeneity will be missed. Consequently, the way to overcome a poor memory (or small level of significance) is to increase the data size (that is, n) so that the probability of non-prediction becomes negligible.

If at least one occurrence in the general context (---) is remembered, then the expected probability of deletion will equal the overall relative frequency of deletion. But as q (the probability of forgetting an occurrence) approaches one, the greater the chances that no prediction at all will be made:

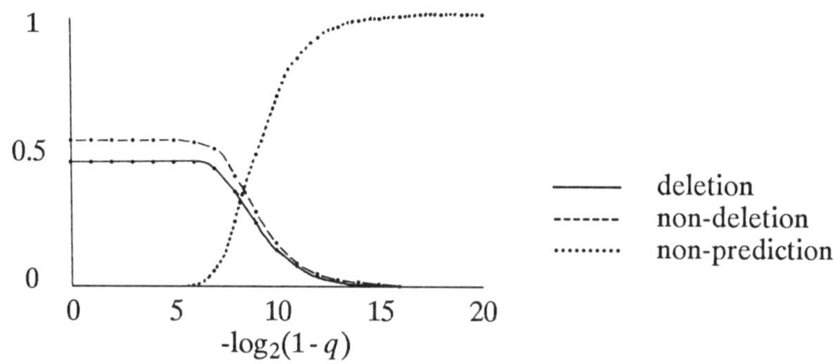

The horizontal axis is logarithmic and each unit increase represents a halving of the probability of remembering an occurrence:

$-\log_2(1-q)$	q	$1-q$
0	0	1
1	0.5	1/2 = 0.5
2	0.75	1/4 = 0.25
3	0.875	1/8 = 0.125
4	0.9375	1/16 = 0.0625
5	0.96875	1/32 = 0.03125
⋮	⋮	⋮

We now consider our data with the first variable specified. Suppose that the given context is *v*--:

CONTEXTUAL VARIABLES			OUTCOMES		
1	2	3	deletion	non-deletion	
v	-	-	55	161	216
c	-	-	117	37	154
			172	198	370

In all there are 216 occurrences of *v*-- in the data set. So as long as at least one of these 216 occurrences is remembered, the given context will occur and will completely determine the predicted outcome. On the other hand, if all 216 occurrences of *v*-- are forgotten, then any of the remaining 154 occurrences of *c*-- can be used to predict the outcome. But if none of these 154 occurrences are remembered either, then no prediction at all is possible. The probability of these three possibilities can be calculated precisely:

$$Pr(\text{deletion}) = (55/216)(1-q^{216}) + (117/154)q^{216}(1-q^{154})$$

$$Pr(\text{non-deletion}) = (161/216)(1-q^{216}) + (37/154)q^{216}(1-q^{154})$$

$$Pr(\text{non-prediction}) = q^{370}$$

As *q* approaches one, the probability of non-prediction overwhelms the probability of the two normal outcomes of deletion and non-deletion:

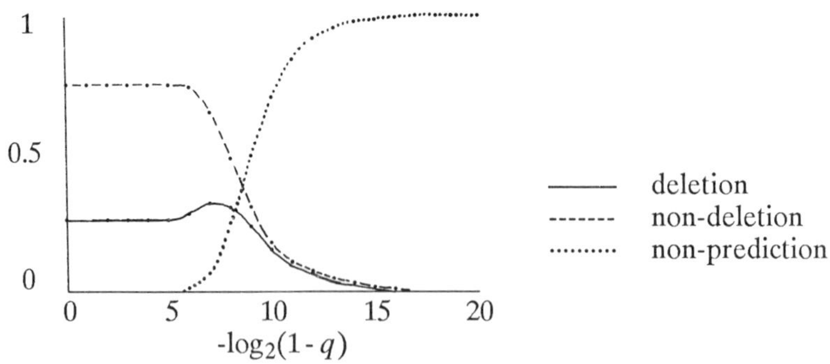

But if we consider only the two cases when we can actually predict an outcome, we see that as q approaches one we obtain the expected probability for the general context (---); namely, 172/370 = 46.5%:

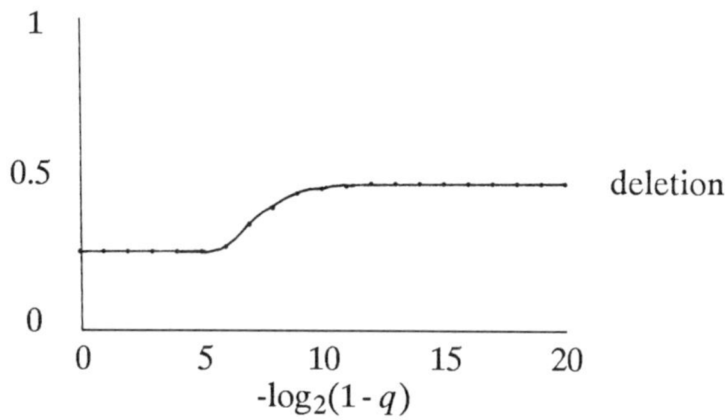

For $q < 0.97$ the given context *v*-- dominates, but when q gets close to one then the general context (---) takes over.

We get more complicated results when we add the second variable to the first, yet the basic overall behavior is the same. As q moves away from zero, the influence of the given context will diminish (depending on the frequency of the given context). Nearby contexts then start to influence the outcome, but finally as q gets close to one, non-predictability overwhelms the system. As an example, consider the given context *vm*-. We first determine the number of occurrences for this given context as well as its subcontexts:

	deletion	non-deletion	
vm-	21	10	31
$v\bar{m}$- (= *vw*-)	34	151	185
$\bar{v}m$- (= *cm*-)	34	6	40
$\bar{v}\bar{m}$- (= *cw*-)	83	31	114
	172	198	370

As long as there is at least one occurrence of *vm*- (the given context), the other subcontexts will have no effect on the predicted outcome. But with no occurrences of the given context (*vm*-), the two nearest subcontexts (*vw*- and *cm*-) will determine the outcome (providing at least one of these two subcontexts actually occurs). However, the influence of these two subcontexts will not be due to their frequency alone, but rather their frequency squared (since our measure of certainty is a quadratic measure). Thus the more frequent subcontext *vw*- has considerably more pointers:

	DATA			NUMBER OF POINTERS: deletion	NUMBER OF POINTERS: non-deletion
vw-	34	151	185	$34 \times 185 = 6290$	$151 \times 185 = 27935$
cm-	34	6	40	$34 \times 40 = 1360$	$6 \times 40 = 240$
				7650	28175

Thus if the given context *vm*- does not occur, then the chances of deletion are substantially reduced. Under such conditions, the nearby subcontext *vw*- will dominate the other nearby subcontext, *cm*-. If neither these two subcontexts nor the given context occurs, then the furthest subcontext *cw*- will determine the outcome (providing it occurs). Finally, if no occurrences at all are remembered, then no prediction will be possible.

For a given value of q (the probability of forgetting an occurrence), we can determine the probability of deletion, non-deletion, and non-prediction:

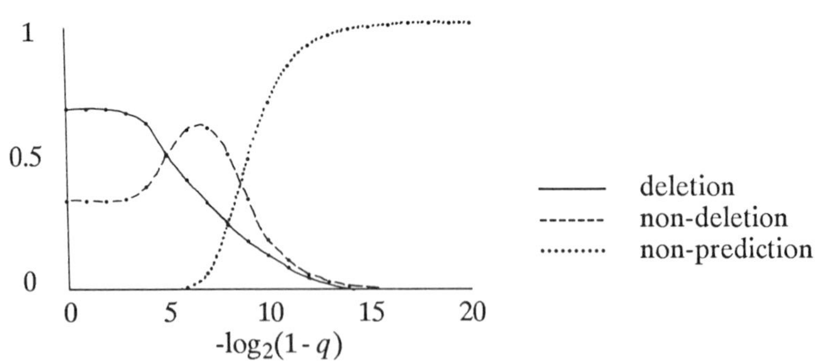

This graph shows that as q moves away from zero, the probability of non-deletion rises considerably, due to the strong influence of the nearby subcontext *vw-*. But as q continues to increase and approaches one, non-predictability overwhelms the system.

But we should also consider what happens when we ignore the case of non-predictability. In the case of a single variable, we saw that the asymptotic probability (as q approaches one) equals the expected probability for the general context (---). In the case of two (or more) variables, this same result holds. For instance, the asymptotic probability of deletion for the context *vm-* is the same 46.5%:

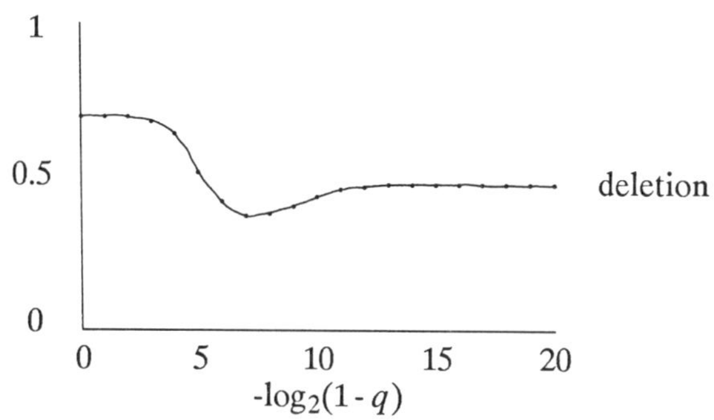

Finally, when we consider Fasold's data in terms of all three variables, we have a number of cases of low frequency. When we try to predict the behavior of infrequent cases, we discover that the predicted behavior is dominated by nearby subcontexts of greater frequency, especially as q (the probability of forgetting an occurrence) moves away from zero. Consider, for instance, the given contexts *cmp* and *vmf*. As q moves away from zero, the predicted behavior of these infrequent contexts (represented by the solid line, ——) quickly matches the behavior of surrounding subcontexts (represented by the dashed line, -------):

cmp (2 occurrences)

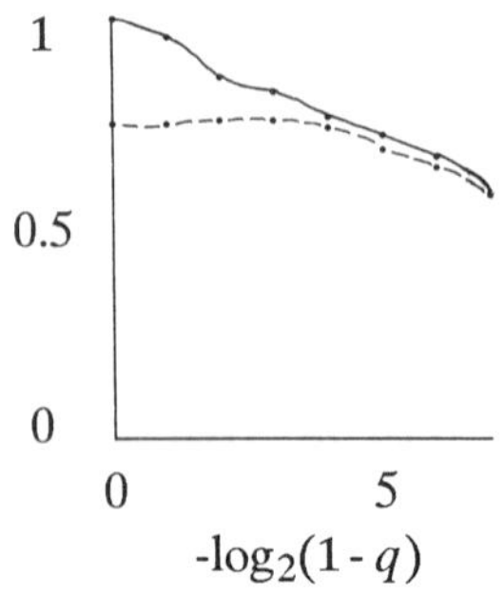

vmf (5 occurrences)

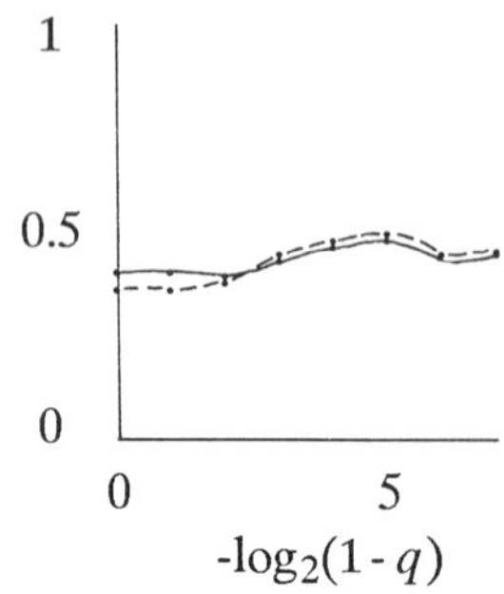

When three variables are specified, it becomes quite difficult to determine the exact relationship between q (the probability of forgetting an occurrence) and the expected probability of deletion. So in this case I have used Monte Carlo methods to estimate the probability of deletion. Each of these estimates is based on a thousand random samples of the data set.[3]

As we expect, the greater the frequency of the given context, the longer it takes for surrounding subcontexts to influence the predicted outcome, as can be seen from the following four examples:

vmp (14 occurrences)

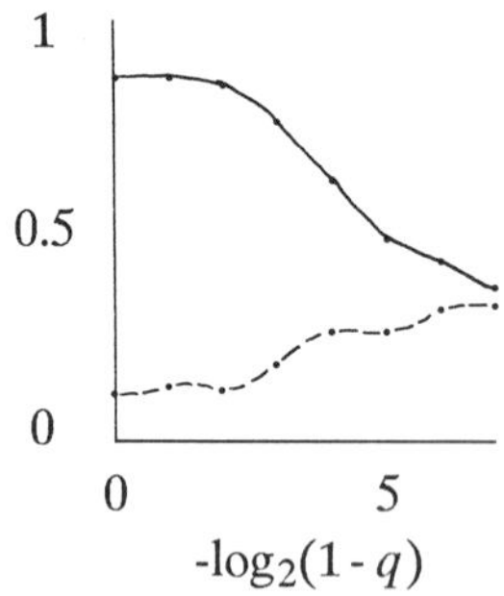

cwf (32 occurrences)

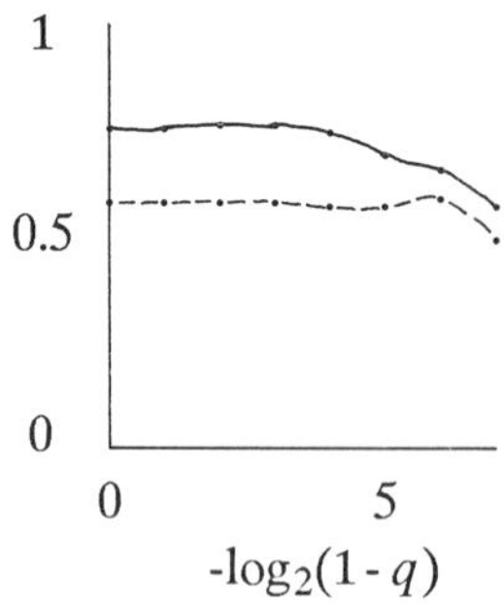

[3] Appendix 3 gives the computer program that I used to make analogical predictions (under conditions of imperfect memory) for Fasold's data.

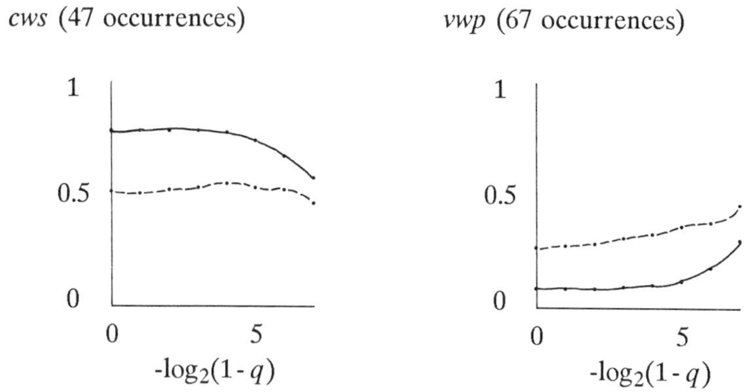

4. Rule Approaches to Language Variation

IN attempting to account for data like Fasold's, variationists have assumed that multivariate effects are simple mathematical functions of single variables (Cedergren and Sankoff 1974:335-336). This is, of course, a very specific assumption and one wonders whether there is any evidence from language learning for such an underlying separation of variables. In addition, there is the question of what mathematical function describes the multivariate effects. For instance, one may ask which model (additive, multiplicative non-application, or multiplicative application) fits the data best – or, equivalently, which parameters should be assigned to a logistic model (Rousseau and Sankoff 1978:57-58,62). Yet there appears to be little evidence for a principled basis on which to choose the appropriate model. The analyst simply selects (on an ad hoc basis) those parameters that fit the data best.

The assumption of variable separation appears to be motivated by the desire to avoid specifying probabilities for every possible combination of variables. (Of course, in an analogical approach there is no need to specify probabilities in order to obtain probabilistic behavior.) This problem is particularly troublesome because there doesn't seem to be any limit to the number of variables that can affect any given non-deterministic phenomenon in language. In other words, there seems to be no end to the variation. This reminds one of the well-known suspicion that completely independent variables are rare, that given enough data almost any two variables can be shown to be dependent to some degree (Hays 1973:752).

As an example of this problem, let us reconsider Guy's discussion of final /t,d/ deletion in English (Guy 1980:5-10). Guy first lists Labov's three main linguistic variables that affect the probability of final /t,d/ deletion. Originally, Labov assigned two variants to two of these linguistic variables and ignored the lesser effect of the third:

1 *grammatical conditioning:* Is the word monomorphemic or bimorphemic?

2 *conditioning by following segment:* Is the segment a vowel or a non-vowel?

3 *conditioning by preceding segment* [not specified in Labov's original study]

Over the years additional studies have shown that each of these variables should be assigned more variants – that additional distinctions are necessary if we want to account for statistically significant effects on final /t,d/ deletion. Guy partitions these three variables more finely:

1 *grammatical conditioning:* Is the word monomorphemic, the past tense of an irregular weak verb (like *deal/dealt*), or the past tense of a regular weak verb (like *seal/sealed*)?

2 *conditioning by following segment:* Is the segment a (true) consonant, a glide, a liquid, a vowel, or a pause?

3 *conditioning by preceding segment:* Is the segment a sibilant, a nonsibilant fricative, a nasal, a stop, or a lateral?

So from an original four-way distinction we now have a potential distribution of seventy-five possibilities ($3 \times 5 \times 5 = 75$).

But this is not all. Other variables have been discovered that affect the probability of final /t,d/ deletion: lexical stress, rate of speech, length of consonant cluster, articulatory complexity of clusters, speech style, and social factors (such as age, sex, social class, race, and geographic background).

Guy rightly observes that this rule of final /t,d/ deletion cannot be reduced to deterministic phenomena (Guy 1980:11). But the history of this example also implies that final /t,d/ deletion cannot be completely described either! There doesn't seem to be any limit to the number of variables that affect final /t,d/ deletion. As more data is collected, more distinctions are discovered. The effect of these additional variables is less important, but they are still statistically significant. It appears as if no complete rule description of final /t,d/ deletion will ever be forthcoming.

But in an analogical approach there is no need to discover the correct description. And in principle there is no need to determine which variables are significant, although given the current memory and processing limitations of computers, some restriction on variable choice is unavoidable. In this book we have been able to specify up to a dozen variables, so in restricting the number of variables we have sought to choose those variables that permit local predictability and allow for maximum differentiation of the data set. But it has not been necessary to decide in advance which of these variables are the "correct" variables.[4]

5. *Sociolinguistic Variation in Arabic*

IN Fasold's data, only three linguistic variables are specified. We now turn to a significantly more complex case of sociolinguistic variation. In colloquial Egyptian Arabic there are two terms of address that mean 'my brother', *ya'axi* and *yaxuuya.* In the following analysis, I use 242 examples of these two terms as collected by Dil Parkinson. In this data, the term *ya'axi* was used 53.7% of the time, yet there are a number of distinct factors that can affect the probability of using one term over the other.[5]

---

[4] See section 3.1 for further discussion of the problem of variable selection.

[5] For a complete list of the Arabic data, see appendix 2.4.

We analyze this data using eight different social and discourse variables:

1-3 the sex, social class, and age of the speaker

4-5 the social class and age of the addressee[6]

6 the speaker's tone of voice

7 the power relationship defined by the social situation

8 the degree of closeness or familiarity between the speaker and the addressee

In the following graph we can see the divergence from the overall mean (53.7%) for each of these variables:

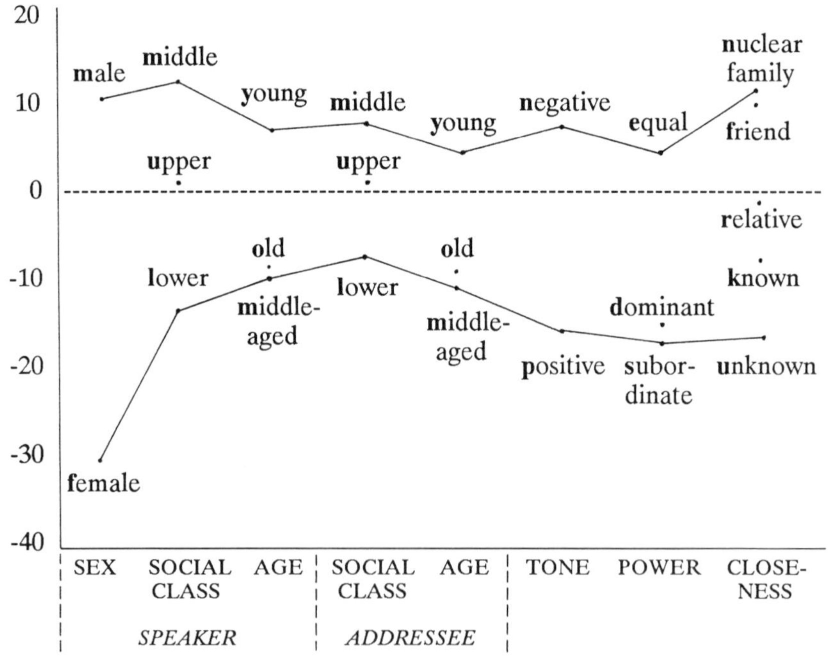

[6] Addressee sex is ignored since both these terms mean 'my brother' and thus require a male addressee.

As we have seen, a rule approach raises the question of how all these variables might work together to predict which form of 'my brother' (*ya'axi* or *yaxuuya*) should be used under various conditions. We might tentatively conclude from the above chart that certain combinations would favor *ya'axi* or *yaxuuya*. Despite numerous attempts by both statisticians and linguistic variationists, there has been little success in devising a rule-based approach for predicting the behavior of non-deterministic multivariate data that would at the same time be conceptually simple and psychologically plausible.

On the other hand, an analogical approach readily predicts the outcome for any given context of non-deterministic variables. Consider, for instance, the given context {flmlmpsu} (that is, a female speaker of the lower class, middle-aged, speaking to a lower-class male, also middle-aged, in a positive tone, the speaker being in a subordinate position, and the addressee unknown to the speaker). There are no occurrences of this context in the data set, yet the analogical approach predicts under various levels of memory retention that we should strongly expect the speaker to use *yaxuuya* rather than *ya'axi*. In the following table we have the predicted probability (in percent) of the outcome *yaxuuya* for {flmlmpsu}. Each probability is based on a hundred Monte Carlo estimates:

LEVEL OF MEMORY RETENTION	PROBABILITY OF *yaxuuya*
1.0	99.9
0.5	99.6
0.25	97.3
0.125	87.8
0.0625	77.5
0.03125	71.1

The non-occurring given context {flmlmpsu} appears in a field where *yaxuuya* rather than *ya'axi* dominates – thus even when memory retention is rather poor (as low as 1/32), the chances of *yaxuuya* being predicted remain quite high.

Now let us consider a given context that occurs in the data, but can be considered exceptional when compared to the data surrounding it – namely, {mmylynek} (that is, a male from the middle-class who is young speaking to a lower-class male who is also young, in a negative tone, the speaker being equal to the addressee, and the addressee a known acquaintance of the speaker's). From the eight variables alone we might naturally expect that the favored form of 'my brother' would be *ya'axi* in such a situation, yet in the data the single occurrence of this form takes *yaxuuya*. Nonetheless, at lower levels of memory retention, we see that in fact *ya'axi* is favored for this given context, but that *yaxuuya* is still quite possible. In the following table we once more have the predicted probability (in percent) of the outcome *ya'axi* for {mmylynek}. As before, each probability is based on a hundred Monte Carlo estimates:

LEVEL OF MEMORY RETENTION	PROBABILITY OF *ya'axi*
1.0	0.0
0.5	34.8
0.25	56.8
0.125	64.7
0.0625	69.8
0.03125	67.6

From a statistical point of view, low levels of memory retention correspond to small levels of significance. This means that for this particular given context ({mmylynek}) the single occurrence of *yaxuuya* is not all that significant when compared with the overall behavior of nearby occurrences. (In fact, we might compare the behavior of {mmylynek} with the twenty-five occurrences of the nearby {mmymynef}, of which eighteen take the outcome *ya'axi*.)

For both of these given contexts there is no need to determine the probabilistic relationship between the variables specified in the given context. Yet the predicted behavior looks "rule governed". In other words, speakers' knowledge of their language is much less direct than a rule approach would suggest. Speakers generally lack the ability to make explicit the rules that govern their behavior. An analogical approach suggests that the reason for this inability is not that the rules are somehow inaccessible, but instead that the rules don't actually exist.

Chapter Five

ANALOGICAL PREDICTIONS OF THE PAST TENSE IN FINNISH

1. An Overview of the Verb Types

IN this chapter I will apply the analogical approach to the past tense in standard Finnish. I first discuss in general terms how the past tense is derived from the present tense stem. Except for one important context, the past tense is completely predictable. For this one non-deterministic context, I discuss the variation that is found in samplings of Finnish texts as well as linguistic descriptions of this variation. I then show how an analogical approach can predict the synchronic behavior of this important class of verbs – and not only for frequent verbs found in textual samplings, but also for rarely occurring verbs. Finally, I show how an analogical approach can account for the complex problem of historical drift in the Finnish past tense.

In this chapter, past tense forms will be predicted in terms of the verb stem (which is equivalent to the present stem). For most verb stems only one past tense form is possible:

(1) Verb stems ending in a short unstressed round vowel add *i* to form the past tense: *sano-* 'say' ~ *sanoi, puhu-* 'speak' ~ *puhui, kysy-* 'ask' ~ *kysyi, säilö-* 'preserve' ~ *säilöi.*

(2) Verb stems ending in a long stressed vowel have in the past tense a diphthongal form of the vowel ending in *i:* *saa-* 'get' ~ *sai, jää-* 'remain' ~ *jäi, myy-* 'sell' ~ *myi* (which also occasionally has an exceptional past tense form, *möi*).

(3) Verb stems ending in *i* have an identical past tense form: *toimi-* 'act' ~ *toimi, ui-* 'swim' ~ *ui, rekisteröi-* 'register' ~ *rekisteröi.*

(4) Verb stems ending in an unstressed vowel immediately followed by a low vowel have a past tense form in which the low vowel is replaced by *si:* *halua-* 'want' ~ *halusi, häviä-* 'disappear' ~ *hävisi, avaa-* 'open' ~ *avasi.*

(5) Verb stems ending in a stressed falling diphthong (a high vowel immediately followed by a mid vowel of the same rounding and backness) have a past tense form ending in the mid vowel immediately followed by *i:* *vie-* 'take' ~ *vei, juo-* 'drink' ~ *joi, syö-* 'eat' ~ *söi.*

(6) The verb stem *käy-* 'visit' has the past tense form *kävi.*

On the other hand, there are three past tense cases that overlap and therefore permit some variation in behavior. In the most general case, if the verb stem ends in a consonant followed by a short unstressed *e, ä,* or *a* (that is, a short unstressed non-high unround vowel, which I will represent by the symbol *Æ*), then that vowel is replaced by *i* in the past tense:

tule- 'come' ~ *tuli*
mainitse- 'mention' ~ *mainitsi*
pitä- 'hold' ~ *piti*
esittä- 'present' ~ *esitti*
muista- 'remember' ~ *muisti*
aloitta- 'begin' ~ *aloitti*

In order to define the domain in the other two cases, we have to add specification to the preceding case:

(i) If the unstressed final *Æ* vowel is immediately preceded by *t* and the *t* is immediately preceded by a resonant (that is, by either a sonorant or a vowel), then the *t* and the following *Æ* vowel are replaced by *si* to form the past tense:

myöntä- 'admit' ~ *myönsi*
rakenta- 'build' ~ *rakensi*
piirtä- 'draw' ~ *piirsi*
ymmärtä- 'understand' ~ *ymmärsi*
kieltä- 'forbid' ~ *kielsi*
sisältä- 'contain' ~ *sisälsi*
tunte- 'feel' ~ *tunsi*
tietä- 'know' ~ *tiesi*
huuta- 'shout' ~ *huusi*
taita- 'know how' ~ *taisi*

(ii) If the final short unstressed vowel is *a* and the verb stem is two syllables long and the first vowel of the first syllable is an unround vowel (that is, *i*, *e*, or *a*),[1] then the final *a* vowel is replaced by *oi* in the past tense:

autta- 'help' ~ *auttoi*
jaka- 'divide' ~ *jakoi*
virkka- 'utter' ~ *virkkoi*
anta- 'give' ~ *antoi*
kaata- 'overturn' ~ *kaatoi*
kasva- 'grow' ~ *kasvoi*
sata- 'rain' ~ *satoi*
paista- 'bake' ~ *paistoi*

---

[1] The *ä* vowel does not occur because of vowel harmony restrictions against *ä* and *a* occurring together in the same morpheme.

I will refer to these three possible past tense cases as *V-i, tV-si,* and *a-oi*. The overlapping domains of these three types can be represented by a Venn diagram:

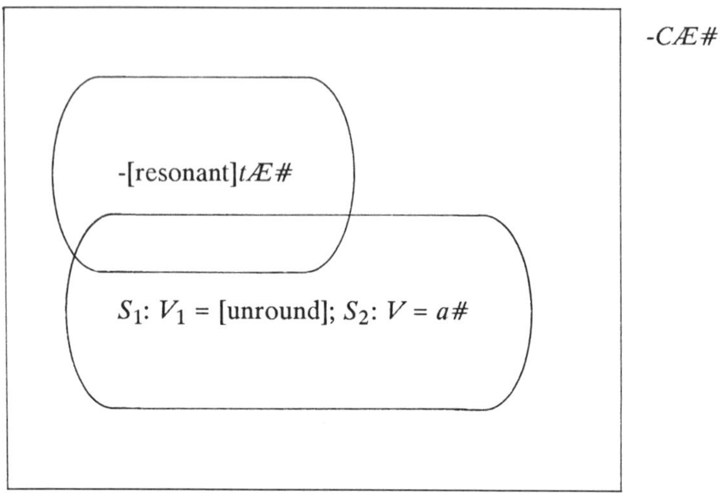

(Here S stands for 'syllable', V for 'vowel', and C for 'consonant'. A symbol of the form X_i stands for the ith X; for instance, S_2 refers to the second syllable, V_1 to the first vowel, and so on. The symbol # represents a morpheme boundary – in this case, the end of the present stem.)

2. *The Past Tense in Standard Finnish*

OF course, for any given verb form found in two or more of these domains, not all possibilities actually occur. In order to make some preliminary observations, let us consider the past tense forms for verbs as they occur in written Finnish. Our examples will be drawn from two statistical studies of Finnish text: (1) Pauli Saukkonen's sampling of 408,301 words from different types of text written in the 1960s, and (2) a sampling of approximately 610,000 words of text from 1975-76 issues of the weekly magazine *Suomen Kuvalehti*. From these sources we first observe the following:

(1) Except in one case, verbs in the domain of the outcome *a-oi* always favor that outcome over the other two outcomes, *V-i* and *tV-si:*

anta-	'give'	*antoi*	222 occurrences
sata-	'rain'	*satoi*	7
laitta-	'prepare'	*laittoi*	6
virkka-	'utter'	*virkkoi*	2

(and thirty-one other verbs); there is only one example of variation and in this case too the outcome *a-oi* dominates:

kaata-	'overturn'	*kaatoi*	14
		kaasi	1

The one exception is *taita-* 'know how', which has thirty-three occurrences of the past tense form *taisi,* but there are no occurrences of *taitoi.*

On the other hand, in those contexts where the outcome *a-oi* is not possible, we note the following:

(2) If the verb stem is of the form $-V^1VtA\#$ (where A stands for any low vowel and V^1 means that the vowel V receives the main stress), we get *V-i* as the outcome unless the verb is quite frequent, in which case we get the outcome *tV-si:*

less frequent:

jäytä-	'gnaw'	*jäyti*	1
kiitä-	'speed'	*kiiti*	1
nouta-	'fetch'	*nouti*	1
sietä-	'tolerate'	*sieti*	1
syytä-	'toss'	*syyti*	1
säätä-	'enact'	*sääti*	2
souta-	'row'	*souti*	4
vuota-	'leak'	*vuoti*	4
hoita-	'tend'	*hoiti*	23

more frequent:

huuta-	'shout'	*huusi*	29
löytä-	'find'	*löysi*	57
pyytä-	'request'	*pyysi*	63
tietä-	'know'	*tiesi*	101

(3) If the verb stem is of the form -V^1*tÆ#*, then only the outcome *V-i* occurs:

itä-	'germinate'	*iti*	2
pote-	'be sick'	*poti*	3
vetä-	'pull'	*veti*	48
pitä-	'hold'	*piti*	345

(4) If the verb stem is of the form -V^1[sonorant]*tA#*, the outcome *V-i* is favored unless the verb is quite frequent, in which case we get *tV-si:*

		VERB FREQUENCY		
less frequent:				
kyntä-	'plow'	10	*kynti*	2
yltä-	'reach'	26	*ylti*	6
			ylsi	1
more frequent:				
murta-	'break'	35	*mursi*	4
lentä-	'fly'	138	*lensi*	28
tunte-	'feel'	982	*tunsi*	81

(5) If the verb stem is of the form -[sonorant]*tA#* and the sonorant is *not* immediately preceded by a short stressed vowel (see the preceding case), then we only get the outcome *tV-si* (if we ignore rare quotes from dialectal speech, such as *kääntivät* 'they turned' and *soveltivat* 'they adapted'):

piirtä-	'draw'	*piirsi*	13	
kieltä-	'forbid'	*kielsi*	14	
työntä-	'push'	*työnsi*	15	
kiertä-	'wind'	*kiersi*	15	
kääntä-	'turn'	*käänsi*	23	(*käänti* 1)
myöntä-	'admit'	*myönsi*	25	
sovelta-	'adapt'	*sovelsi*	1	(*sovelti* 1)
sisältä-	'contain'	*sisälsi*	15	
rakenta-	'build'	*rakensi*	16	
ymmärtä-	'understand'	*ymmärsi*	21	

3. Variation in the Past Tense

IN this chapter I wish to account for two kinds of information that describe the competition among these past tense forms: (1) the current use and tendencies in the language, and (2) the historical development. From a synchronic perspective, I wish to account at least qualitatively for the results in Paunonen 1973. In this article Paunonen discusses the competition between the two outcomes *V-i* and *tV-si,* first in terms of his own intuitions, then in terms of an experiment he conducted. According to his intuitions (1973:291), there is a continuum of choice between these two outcomes:

> only *tV-si* possible: *tiesi, huusi, pyysi, kielsi, piirsi, mursi*
>
> *tV-si* favored, but *V-i* possible: *suolsi* (~ *suolti*) [*suolta-* 'let glide']
>
> both equally possible: *ylti* ~ *ylsi, souti* ~ *sousi*
>
> *V-i* favored, but *tV-si* possible: *vuoti* (~ *vuosi*), *kiiti* (~ *kiisi*)
>
> only *V-i* possible: *hoiti, hyyti* [*hyytä-* 'clot'], *jääti* [*jäätä-* 'freeze'], *veti, piti*

For verbs in the category $\text{-}V^1VtA\#$, Mauno Koski has provided a similar list (Karlsson 1982:347):

only *tV-si* possible: *tiesi, löysi, huusi, pyysi*

both equally possible: *kiiti* ~ *kiisi*

V-i favored, but *tV-si* possible: *hyyti* (~ *hyysi*), *souti* (~ *sousi*), *vuoti* (~ *vuosi*), *hääti* (~ *hääsi*) [*häätä-* 'evict'], *liiti* (~ *liisi*) [*liitä-* 'glide'], *sääti* (~ *sääsi*)

only *V-i* possible: *hoiti, jouti* [*jouta-* 'have time'], *jääti, jäyti, syyti, sieti, suoti* [*suota-* 'ooze'], *nouti*

From Paunonen's and Koski's judgements, we may conclude that for the category $-V^1VtA\#$ four frequent verbs clearly favor the outcome *tV-si* (*tietä-* 'know', *pyytä-* 'request', *löytä-* 'find', and *huuta-* 'shout'); in all other cases the favored outcome is *V-i* with varying degrees of acceptability for the outcome *tV-si*.

Paunonen also outlines different circumstances that could affect the choice of outcome: the forms *tieti, huuti, hoisi,* and *jääsi* seem to be possible as occasional slips of the tongue, but *vesi* and *pisi* seem completely impossible, "even as slips of the tongue" (1973:291). In addition, Paunonen (1973:291) and Koski (see Karlsson 1982:347) would judge some forms as dialectal; for example, *piirti, murti, pyyti, huuti, löyti,* and *syysi.*

In his experiment Paunonen (1973:292-293) had thirty-six first-year university students judge various past tense forms as being (1) neither natural nor possible, (2) not very natural but possible, and (3) quite natural and possible. In the following chart, we see the results of his experiment:

WORD	GLOSS	*tV-si*	*V-i*	DIFFERENCE
tietä-	'know'	3.00	1.17	1.83
löytä-	'find'	3.00	1.56	1.44
rientä-	'hasten'	2.97	1.54	1.43
huuta-	'shout'	2.97	1.56	1.41
piirtä-	'draw'	2.97	1.64	1.33
kääntä-	'turn'	2.94	1.67	1.27
työntä-	'push'	3.00	1.75	1.25
myöntä-	'admit'	3.00	1.78	1.22
ääntä-	'pronounce'	2.94	1.75	1.19

pyytä-	'request'	3.00	1.83	1.17
kieltä-	'forbid'	2.97	1.83	1.14
lentä-	'fly'	3.00	1.86	1.14
siirtä-	'move'	2.92	1.94	0.98
murta-	'break'	3.00	2.06	0.94
kiertä-	'wind'	2.78	1.86	0.92
kiiltä-	'glisten'	2.89	2.00	0.89
hiertä-	'grind'	2.92	2.03	0.89
puolta-	'support'	2.97	2.11	0.86
puurta-	'trudge'	2.72	2.06	0.66
uurta-	'groove'	2.61	2.00	0.61
siintä-	'be dimly visible'	2.81	2.33	0.48
suolta-	'let glide'	2.69	2.36	0.33
souta-	'row'	2.33	2.61	-0.28
kiitä-	'speed'	2.26	2.63	-0.37
hyytä-	'clot'	2.00	2.61	-0.61
vuota-	'leak'	1.97	2.67	-0.70
häätä-	'evict'	1.86	2.66	-0.80
yltä-	'reach'	1.86	2.81	-0.95
liitä-	'glide'	1.75	2.72	-0.97
säätä-	'enact'	1.92	2.92	-1.00
jäätä-	'freeze'	1.40	2.47	-1.07
syytä-	'toss'	1.64	2.72	-1.08
jäytä-	'gnaw'	1.83	2.92	-1.09
hoita-	'tend'	1.71	2.81	-1.10
nouta-	'fetch'	1.67	2.89	-1.22
sorta-	'oppress'	1.60	2.86	-1.26
jouta-	'have time'	1.53	2.81	-1.28
sieta-	'tolcrate'	1.46	2.94	-1.48
kyntä-	'plow'	1.39	2.92	-1.53
pitä-	'hold'	1.00	3.00	-2.00
vetä-	'pull'	1.00	3.00	-2.00

A value of 3.00 for a past tense form means that all thirty-six students judged this item as completely acceptable, while a value of 1.00 means that all thirty-six students rejected the item; most forms have a composite value somewhere along the continuum between one and three.

A second kind of problem that confronts us is the historical development, in particular the question of why so many past tense forms ending in *si* have been replaced with *ti*. In Proto-Balto-Finnic the dental stop *t* was palatalized to *tś* when immediately followed by *i* (except when preceded by a dental or palatal obstruent). Later this palatal affricate ended up merging with *s*. According to the standard historical reconstruction, there are a good number of verbs that originally had past tense forms ending in *si* (such as *pitä-* 'hold', *vetä-* 'pull', *pote-* 'be sick', *hoita-* 'tend', and *sorta-* 'oppress'), yet now in Finnish these verbs definitely prefer past tense forms ending in *ti*.

4. Properties of an Analogically Predicted Past Tense Form

IN applying the analogical approach to the Finnish past tense, I first constructed a data set composed of all two-syllable verb stems ending in a short unstressed *e, ä,* or *a* vowel that had at least one past tense occurrence in either the Saukkonen or *Suomen Kuvalehti* textual studies. In all, there were 173 verbs in the resulting data set: 117 with the *V-i* outcome, 36 with the *a-oi* outcome, and 20 with the *tV-si* outcome. There were only four verbs with statistically variant past tense forms in the two studies; in addition to the variants already mentioned (*yltä-* 'reach', *kaata-* 'overturn', and *kääntä-* 'turn'), *lähte-* 'depart' had 203 occurrences of the regular past tense form *lähti* and 13 of the exceptional *läksi*. For each of these four verbs, I assigned the most frequent outcome: *ylti, kaatoi, käänsi,* and *lähti.*[2]

In order to determine the contexts for a given form, phonetic similarity must be defined. For this data set phonetic similarity is defined in terms of phonemic and syllabic identity (as discussed in section 3.1). Nonetheless, this phonetic analysis is only preliminary and the data set needs to be extended to words longer than two syllables.

---

[2] For a complete list of the 173 Finnish verbs and their outcomes, see appendix 2.5.

Each verb in the list was analyzed in terms of the following ten variables:

1 the word-initial phoneme

2 the first vowel in the word

3 whether the first vowel is immediately followed by another vowel in the same syllable (V) or not (ø)

4 the following vowel in the same syllable, if it exists (see variable 3); if not, the non-specification symbol (=)

5 whether the vowel(s) of the first syllable are followed by a sonorant in the same syllable (S) or not (ø)

6 the following sonorant in the same syllable, if it exists (see variable 5); if not, the non-specification symbol (=)

7 whether the vowel(s) of the first syllable are followed by an obstruent in the same syllable (O) or not (ø)

8 the following obstruent in the same syllable, if it exists (see variable 7); if not, the non-specification symbol (=)

9 the last consonant in the word

10 the last vowel in the word

We give the variable specification for the following verbs (representative of the various possibilities for two-syllable verbs):[3]

aja-	'drive'	aaø=ø=ø=ja
kartta-	'avoid'	kaø=SrOtta
maksa-	'pay'	maø=ø=Oksa
jäytä-	'gnaw'	jäVyø=ø=tä
kieltä-	'forbid'	kiVeSlø=tä

[3] For a complete list of the variable specifications for the 173 verbs, see appendix 2.5.

Now let us consider the analogical set that was generated for a verb not in the data set – namely, *häätä-* 'evict':[4]

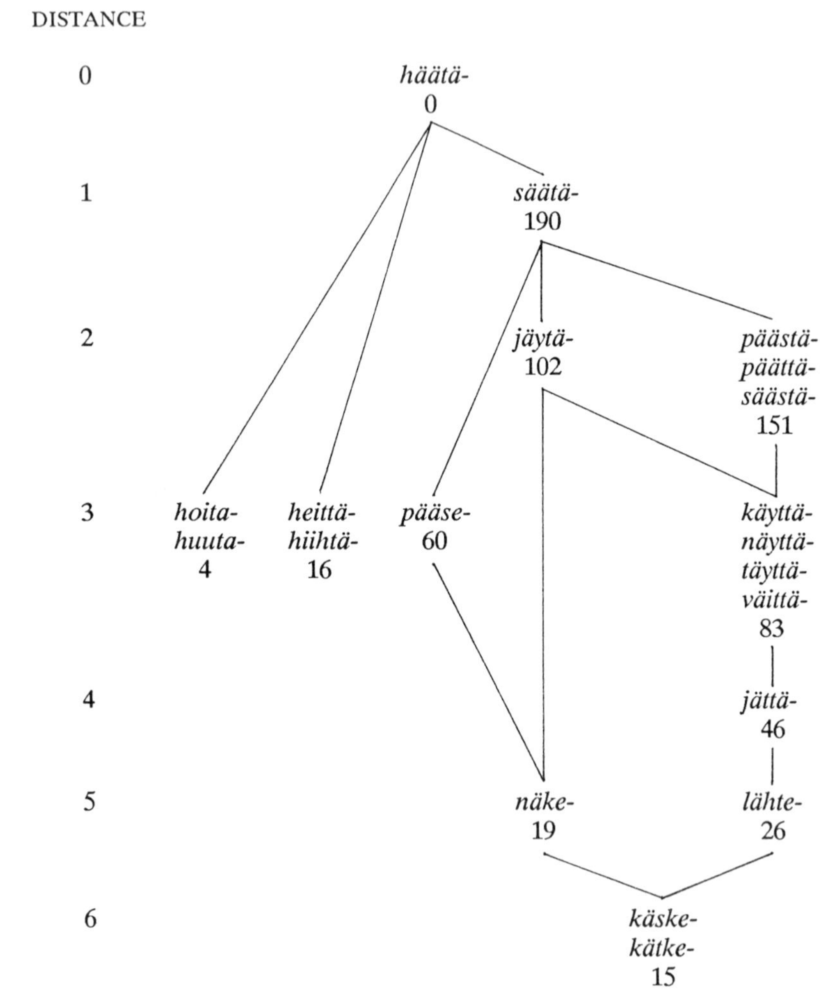

---

[4] For the meanings of the analogical words, see appendix 2.5.

We make several observations about this diagram:

(1) The distance specifies the number of phonetic differences between the connected forms. For instance, the difference between *häätä-* and *päästä-* 'let go' is two: one phonemic difference (*h* is phonemically distinct from *p*) and one syllabic difference (an obstruent is inserted in *päästä-*).

(2) All of the contexts in the analogical set are deterministic in behavior except for the group that contains the verbs *hoita-* 'tend' and *huuta-* 'shout'. This group is non-deterministic since *hoita-* takes the outcome *V-i* while *huuta-* takes the outcome *tV-si*. Note also that this non-deterministic group of contexts is unobstructed: no other occurrences intervene between it and the non-occurring *häätä-*.

(3) Under each group of verbs the number of pointers for each verb in the group is specified. Since all the occurrences in the analogical set take the *V-i* outcome except for *huuta-* 'shout', there are 1294 pointers with the outcome *V-i*, but only four with the outcome *tV-si*. Thus the probability of randomly selecting the outcome *V-i* is nearly one:

$$Pr(V\text{-}i\,|\,h\ddot{a}\ddot{a}t\ddot{a}\text{-}) = 1294/1298 = 0.997$$

(4) In this analogical set there is a strong gang effect for the verbs that have *ä* as the first vowel and do not begin with *h*. In fact, this phonetic characterization holds for fifteen out of the nineteen verbs in the analogical set. On the other hand, the exceptionally behaving *huuta-* 'shout' sharply restricts the gang effect for the four remaining verbs (all of which begin with *h* and do not have *ä* as the first vowel).

(5) For the fifteen verbs with a pronounced gang effect there is an inverse exponential relationship between the distance from *häätä-* and the number of pointers in the analogical set:

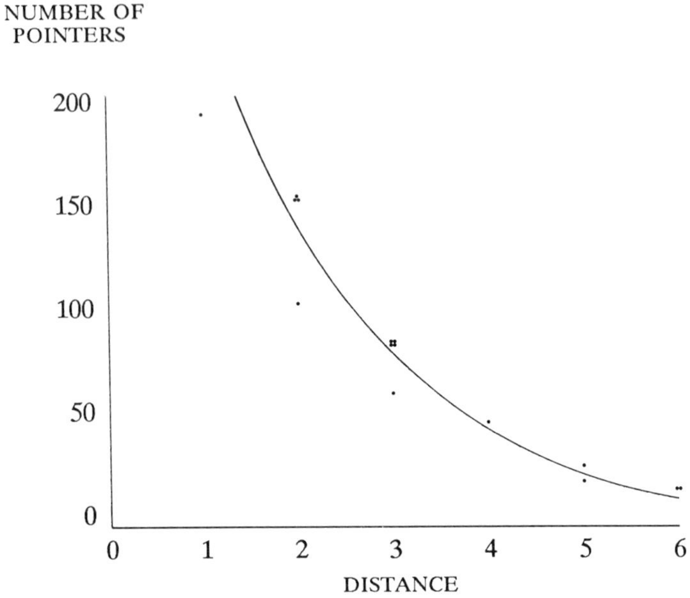

In general, the closer an occurring verb is to the given verb, the greater the chances that the occurring verb will serve as the analogical example for predicting the behavior of the given verb.

5. Predicting the Past Tense for Infrequent Verbs

NOW let us consider the results of applying this analogical approach to verbs which were not in the data set. In general, these verbs occurred in the two textual studies but not in the past tense. Verbs that did not appear at all in the samplings are marked with an asterisk (*). We categorize the verbs according to possible outcomes and syllabic structure. All predicted probabilities (in this section as well as the next) are given in percent.

only *V-i* and *a-oi* as possible outcomes:

S_1: $V_1 = a$

		$Pr(V\text{-}i)$	$Pr(a\text{-}oi)$
ahta-	'pack'	0	100
kalva-	'prey on'	4.3	95.7
kasta-	'baptize'	3.5	96.5
lappa-	'haul'	0.8	99.2
maitta-	'please'	0.2	99.8
paukka-	'crack'	1.5	98.5
mausta-	'season'	0.7	99.3
	average	1.6	98.4

The prediction for *mausta-* 'season' assumes that this verb is two syllables long; historically this verb is three syllables long (*ma.us.ta-*, compare *maku* 'taste') and the *Nykysuomen sanakirja* (*NSSK*) gives only the past tense form *mausti* – that is, the outcome *V-i*.)

S_1: $V_1 = i$

		$Pr(V\text{-}i)$	$Pr(a\text{-}oi)$
viuhka-	'swish'	93.7	6.3

The *NSSK* gives only the *V-i* outcome for *viuhka-*.

all three outcomes possible:

-a^1V[sonorant]*ta*

		$Pr(V\text{-}i)$	$Pr(a\text{-}oi)$	$Pr(tV\text{-}si)$
kaarta-	'swerve'	0	48.6	51.4
saarta-	'surround'	0.1	41.9	57.9
	average	0.1	45.3	54.7

-a^1Vta

		$Pr(V\text{-}i)$	$Pr(a\text{-}oi)$	$Pr(tV\text{-}si)$
raata-	'toil'	0	99.6	0.4

The *NSSK* lists both *a-oi* and *tV-si* as possible outcomes for the first two verbs (*kaarta-* 'swerve' and *saarta-* 'surround'), but only *a-oi* for *raata-* 'toil'. Even though all these verbs can, in theory, take all three outcomes, the analogical approach predicts the clear difference in behavior between those verbs that have a sonorant immediately preceding the *t* and those that don't.

only *V-i* and *tV-si* as possible outcomes:

-$V^1tÆ\#$

		$Pr(V\text{-}i)$	$Pr(tV\text{-}si)$
kute-	'spawn'	99.8	0.2
päte-	'be valid'	100	0
**syte-*	'chip'	100	0
	average	99.9	0.1

-$V^1VtA\#$

		$Pr(V\text{-}i)$	$Pr(tV\text{-}si)$
häätä-	'evict'	99.7	0.3
liitä-	'glide'	98.6	1.4
**jäätä-*	'freeze'	100	0
jouta-	'have time'	100	0
suota-	'ooze'	100	0
hyytä-	'clot'	75.0	25.0
	average	95.6	4.4

For *hyytä-* 'clot', 18.8% of the analogical set is due to *pyytä-* 'request', which takes the *tV-si* outcome.

-V^1[sonorant]*tÆ#*

		Pr(*V-i*)	*Pr*(*tV-si*)
**entä-*	'hurry'	50.0	50.0
sorta-	'oppress'	94.1	5.9

The *o* vowel accounts for 91.2% of the analogical set for *sorta-* 'oppress'. And in the data the outcome *V-i* is strongly favored over the *tV-si* outcome when the first vowel is *o*. In addition, the *NSSK* lists *sorta-* as taking the *V-i* outcome – which is essentially what the analogical approach predicts.

-V^1V[sonorant]*tA#*

		Pr(*V-i*)	*Pr*(*tV-si*)
hiertä-	'grind'	0.9	99.1
juonta-	'direct'	7.4	92.6
kiiltä-	'glisten'	11.9	88.1
lientä-	'soothe'	0.4	99.6
mieltä-	'conceive'	0	100
muunta-	'transform'	3.8	96.2
puolta-	'support'	6.2	93.8
puurta-	'trudge'	5.8	94.2
siintä-	'be dimly visible'	0	100
suolta-	'let glide'	8.6	91.4
uurta-	'groove'	1.6	98.4
viertä-	'slope'	1.9	98.1
viiltä-	'slash'	5.8	94.2
ääntä-	'pronounce'	0	100
	average	3.9	96.1

From these results we can rank the predictably consistent categories according to their probability (given in percent) of allowing less frequent outcomes:

(1) -V^1*tÆ#*; *a-oi* not possible 0.1
(*kute-*, *päte-*, *syte-*)

(2) S_1: $V_1 = a$; *tV-si* not possible 1.6
(*ahta-*, *kalva-*, *kasta-*, . . .)

(3) -V^1V[sonorant]$tA\#$; *a-oi* not possible 3.9
(*hiertä-*, *juonta-*, *kiiltä-*, . . .)

(4) -$V^1VtA\#$; *a-oi* not possible 4.4
(*hyytä-*, *häätä-*, *liitä-*, . . .)

For these infrequent verbs, we can compare the predicted probability of the *tV-si* outcome with the results from Paunonen's experiment:

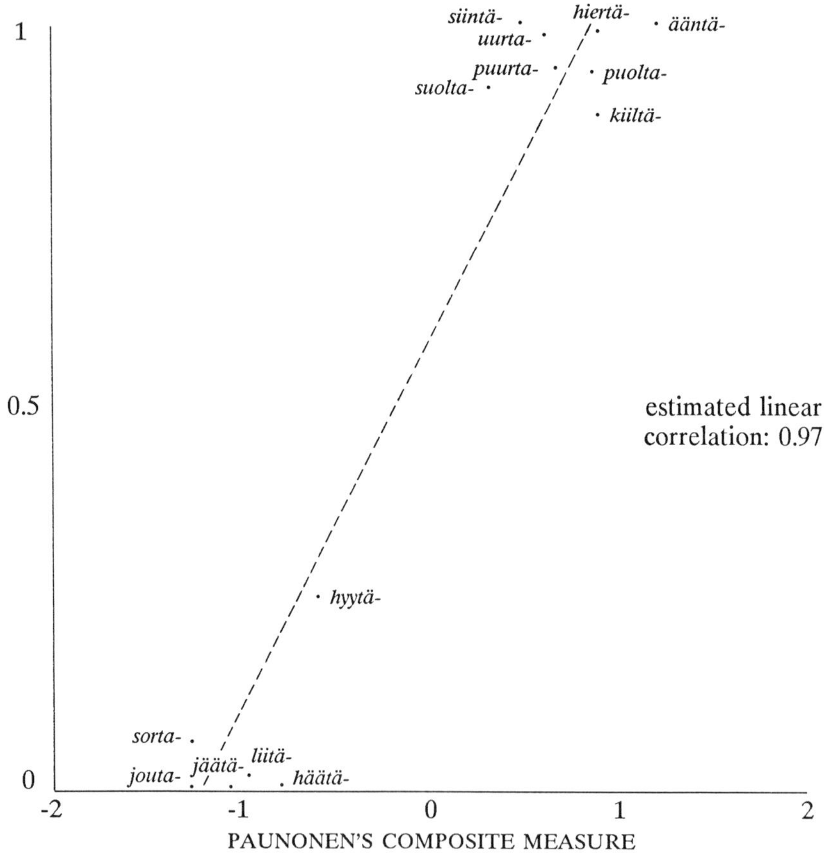

6. Predicting the Past Tense for Verbs in the Data Set

WE now consider what happens when the given verb is one of the verbs in the data set. If the past tense form of such a given verb is remembered, then the analogical probability of selecting that outcome is always one. The more interesting question then is what happens when the past tense form is not remembered. In such a case, the analogical approach will predict a past tense form according to the behavior of the verbs surrounding the given verb. If the surrounding verbs behave like the given verb, then the most frequently predicted outcome will remain the same. In such a case we say that the past tense of the verb is regular. But if the surrounding verbs behave differently, then the given verb is isolated; and under conditions of imperfect memory the predicted past tense will be different. In such a case, we say that the past tense of the given verb is exceptional. In other words, if an exceptional past tense form is not remembered, it will be regularized.

We now apply the analogical approach to the verbs in the data set. Exceptional verbs are marked with an exclamation point(!). As before, we categorize the verbs according to possible outcomes and syllabic structure. We also determine the gang effect for each verb in the data set, and for each category we rank the verbs according to this measure. (The gang effects equals $-\log_2 f$, where f is the fraction of pointers in the analogical set that point to the given context – that is, f is the analogical effect of the given context.[5])

Interestingly, every exceptional verb except one (*kyntä-* 'plow') has a gang effect significantly less than one while every regular verb has a gang effect significantly greater than one. Generally speaking, if the given context is a regular verb, then the analogical effect of the given context is less than one half, but if the given context is an exceptional verb, then the analogical effect of the given context is greater than one half. Thus $f = 1/2$ serves as a convenient boundary between regular and exceptional behavior.

---

[5] See section 3.3 for the definition of the gang effect.

only *V-i* and *a-oi* as possible outcomes:

S_1: $V_1 = a$

		GANG EFFECT	*Pr*(*V-i*)	*Pr*(*a-oi*)
pala-	'burn'	3.84	10.9	89.1
vala-	'cast (metal)'	3.80	1.0	99.0
jaka-	'divide'	3.69	3.5	96.5
aja-	'drive'	3.59	0	100
katta-	'roof'	3.52	3.0	97.0
mahta-	'be capable of'	3.52	2.8	97.2
paina-	'weigh'	3.40	1.2	98.8
kasva-	'grow'	3.38	16.7	83.3
laitta-	'prepare'	3.67	7.3	92.7
laula-	'sing'	3.35	6.5	93.5
maista-	'taste'	3.34	1.8	98.2
taitta-	'break (in two)'	3.34	4.8	95.2
jatka-	'continue'	3.34	10.2	89.8
tappa-	'kill'	3.33	0.8	99.2
paista-	'bake'	3.33	2.7	97.3
naura-	'laugh'	3.33	9.8	90.2
kaiva-	'dig'	3.27	0.2	99.8
autta-	'help'	3.25	2.9	97.1
vaihta-	'(ex)change'	3.25	7.4	92.6
jauha-	'grind'	3.23	1.0	99.0
kaihta-	'shun'	3.21	3.9	96.1
haista-	'smell' [trans.]	3.20	1.6	98.4
jaksa-	'have strength'	3.19	0.4	99.6
saatta-	'accompany'	3.15	9.7	90.3
maksa-	'pay'	3.12	0	100
raasta-	'grate'	3.08	2.5	97.5
paahta-	'scorch'	3.07	0	100
haasta-	'summon'	3.00	0	100
maltta-	'have patience'	2.77	4.3	95.7
alka-	'begin'	2.72	18.8	81.2
kartta-	'avoid'	2.68	0	100
		average	4.4	95.6

This category (S_1: $V_1 = a$) is a nice example of how phonetically similar verbs cluster in the ranking.

S_1: $V_1 = i$

		GANG EFFECT	*Pr*(*V-i*)	*Pr*(*a-oi*)
!*virkka-*	'utter'	0.17	95.4	4.6

all three outcomes possible:

		GANG EFFECT	*Pr*(*V-i*)	*Pr*(*a-oi*)	*Pr*(*tV-si*)
sata-	'rain'	2.60	21.0	78.4	0.6
kanta-	'carry'	1.87	8.4	91.3	0.3
kaata-	'overturn'	1.81	0.7	98.6	0.7
anta-	'give'	1.68	0	100	0
!*taita-*	'know how'	0.46	0.2	99.5	0.3

only *V-i* and *tV-si* as possible outcomes:

-V[1]*tÆ#*

		GANG EFFECT	*Pr*(*V-i*)	*Pr*(*tV-si*)
pote-	'be sick'	4.07	100	0
kyte-	'smolder'	4.07	99.9	0.1
pitä-	'hold'	3.80	99.3	0.7
vetä-	'pull'	3.80	99.8	0.2
itä-	'germinate'	3.73	100	0
		average	99.8	0.2

$-V^1VtA\#$

		PAST TENSE FREQUENCY	GANG EFFECT	*Pr*(*V-i*)	*Pr*(*tV-si*)
hoita-	'tend'	23	3.16	98.8	1.2
souta-	'row'	4	3.06	100	0
nouta-	'fetch'	1	2.99	100	0
kiitä-	'speed'	1	2.70	94.3	5.7
säätä-	'enact'	2	2.35	96.9	3.1
sietä-	'tolerate'	1	2.15	70.3	29.7
jäytä-	'gnaw'	1	2.11	97.0	3.0
syytä-	'toss'	1	2.01	88.1	11.9
vuota-	'leak'	4	1.46	80.2	19.8
!*pyytä-*	'request'	63	0.49	97.2	2.8
!*tietä-*	'know'	101	0.43	98.8	1.2
!*huuta-*	'shout'	29	0.42	98.6	1.4
!*löytä-*	'find'	57	0.05	92.2	7.8
			average	93.3	6.7

Only the four most frequent verbs are exceptional and isolated. Their high frequency has prevented them from being regularized in standard Finnish.

$-V^1$[sonorant]$tÆ\#$

		VERB FREQUENCY	GANG EFFECT	*Pr*(*V-i*)	*Pr*(*tV-si*)
!*kyntä-*	'plow'	10	1.72	33.7	66.3
yltä-	'reach'	26	1.51	95.7	4.3
!*murta-*	'break'	35	0.76	67.7	32.3
!*lentä-*	'fly'	138	0.50	99.7	0.3
!*tunte-*	'feel'	982	0.43	99.2	0.8

Again, the three most frequent verbs are exceptional and isolated. In this category ($-V^1$[sonorant]$tÆ\#$), where the stressed vowel is short, there is an obvious tendency towards regularizing the *V-i* outcome. This was also seen in the earlier analysis of the verbs *sorta-* 'oppress' and *entä-* 'hurry'.) But the predicted behavior of *kyntä-* 'plow' seems to be an exception to this generalization. In fact, this verb is the only exceptional verb that has a gang effect greater than one. According to the *NSSK* the normal outcome for this verb is *V-i,* although *tV-si* is listed as a less frequent possibility. And in the textual studies of standard Finnish, only *kynti* is found. Our analogical predictions are based on phonetic similarity and our results would indicate that phonetic similarity is definitely the deciding factor in predicting the past tense in Finnish. But there is another factor – homophone avoidance – which possibly plays a role in determining the past tense of the verb *kyntä-* 'plow'. The homophony comes from the verb *kynsi-* 'scratch', which has the past tense form *kynsi.* This verb can only take this one past tense form since the verb stem ends in *i* – see verb type (3) at the very beginning of this chapter. On the other hand, *kyntä-* 'plow' can theoretically take either *kynti* or *kynsi* as the past tense form. So to avoid possible confusion in the past tense, speakers prefer the unambiguous *kynti* as the past tense of *kyntä-*.

-V^1V[sonorant]*tA*#

		GANG EFFECT	*Pr*(*V-i*)	*Pr*(*tV-si*)
kiertä-	'wind'	1.83	0	100
rientä-	'hasten'	1.82	6.7	93.3
siirtä-	'move'	1.80	34.4	65.6
piirtä-	'draw'	1.80	4.5	95.5
kieltä-	'forbid'	1.76	2.8	97.2
kääntä-	'turn'	1.73	2.5	97.5
työntä-	'push'	1.72	0	100
myöntä-	'admit'	1.71	0.6	99.4
pyörtä-	'turn back'	1.70	0	100
vääntä-	'twist'	1.68	24.1	75.9
kuulta-	'shine faintly'	1.31	7.1	92.9
huolta-	'maintain'	1.25	32.8	67.2
		average	9.6	90.4

Even though this last category ($-V^1V$[sonorant]*tA#*) favors the *tV-si* outcome, there is some possibility of getting the more general outcome *V-i*.

This potential weakness also shows up when we rank the predictably consistent categories according to their probability (given in percent) of allowing leakage:

(1)	$-V^1$*tÆ#*; *a-oi* not possible (*itä-*, *pote-*, *pitä-*, . . .)	0.24
(2)	S_1: $V_1 = a$; *tV-si* not possible (*maista-*, *katta-*, *paista-*, . . .)	3.44
(3)	$-V^1V$*tA#*; *a-oi* not possible (*hoita-*, *souta-*, *nouta-*, . . .)	6.45
(4)	$-V^1V$[sonorant]*tA#*; *a-oi* not possible (*kieltä-*, *piirtä-*, *kiertä-*, . . .)	9.16

In fact, there are Finnish dialects in which this last class of verbs has taken on this regular *V-i* outcome (Rapola 1966:236-237). On the other hand, there is apparently no tendency for the first verb class to replace the *V-i* past tense by *tV-si*.

7. Historical Drift of the Past Tense

FINALLY we turn to the question of why verbs in the category $-V^1(V)$*tÆ#* have historically tended to shift from past tense forms ending in *si* to *ti*, leaving only a handful of frequent exceptions when the vowel is long. In order to investigate this problem I changed the appropriate outcomes in the data set to reflect the original situation as reconstructed by Finnish historical linguists. This involved the following changes in eighteen verbs:

(1) Every verb of the form $-V^1$([resonant])*tÆ#* was given the outcome *tV-si* unless the verb could potentially take the *a-oi* outcome. This involved changing the outcome of sixteen verbs in the data set: *hoita-* 'tend', *itä-* 'germinate', *jäytä-* 'gnaw', *kiitä-* 'speed', *kyntä-* 'plow', *kyte-* 'smolder', *nouta-* 'fetch', *pitä-* 'hold', *pote-* 'be sick', *sietä-* 'tolerate',

souta- 'row', *syytä-* 'toss', *säätä-* 'enact', *vetä-* 'pull', *vuota-* 'leak', and *yltä-* 'reach'.

(2) All verbs that can potentially take the *a-oi* outcome are given that outcome. This required only one verb to have its outcome changed: *taita-* 'know how' (from *tV-si* to *a-oi*).

(3) The verb *lähte-* 'depart' is given its historical past tense form, the highly exceptional *läksi* rather than the regular past tense form *lähti*. Thus the outcome *V-i* is replaced by *hte-ksi*.

I refer to this revised data set as the primitive data set.[6]

I then developed the following procedure for deriving a stable data set from a given (primitive) data set:

REPEAT UNTIL NO CHANGES OCCUR IN THE DATA SET:
(I) FOR EACH ITEM LISTED IN THE DATA SET:
(A) DETERMINE THE ANALOGICAL SET UNDER
THE FOLLOWING CONDITIONS OF IMPERFECT MEMORY:
(1) THE BEHAVIOR OF THE GIVEN ITEM
IS NOT REMEMBERED,
(2) BUT THE BEHAVIOR OF EVERY OTHER ITEM
IN THE DATA SET IS REMEMBERED;
(B) DETERMINE WHICH OUTCOME IN THE ANALOGICAL SET
OCCURS MOST FREQUENTLY (SELECTION BY PLURALITY);
(II) FOR EACH ITEM LISTED IN THE DATA SET:
IF THE PREDICTED OUTCOME IS DIFFERENT
FROM THE OUTCOME LISTED IN THE DATA SET,
THEN CHANGE THE LISTED OUTCOME
TO AGREE WITH THE PREDICTED OUTCOME.

In essence, this procedure regularizes exceptional items until stability is reached.

I then applied this procedure to the primitive data set to see if there might be any historical drift away from the original situation in Finnish

---

[6] For a summary of the changes made to derive the primitive data set, see appendix 2.5.

towards the current language. And what I discovered in the first run through this procedure was that only one of the eighteen verbs had a predicted outcome different from its original outcome (namely, *lähte-* 'depart' – for which the highly exceptional *hte-ksi* outcome was regularized to *V-i*). In accordance with the above procedure, I then changed the listed outcome of *lähte-* to *V-i*. But in the second run through the procedure, no change at all occurred. In fact, there was no change at all in the predicted probabilities for any of these eighteen verbs (which simply means that *lähte-* is quite isolated from the other seventeen verbs). I concluded from this result that there is no inclination (based on phonetic similarity) for the original *tV-si* outcome to be replaced by the regular outcome *V-i* in any of the sixteen verbs of the form -V^1([resonant])*tÆ#*.

I next tried to determine the effect that semantic similarity might have on the historical development. The verb *taita-* 'know how' is historically supposed to have the past tense form *taitoi,* yet in Finnish dialects, Old Finnish, and standard Finnish we only find evidence of *taisi.* The traditional explanation is that this verb is semantically very close to *tietä-* 'know', which takes the past tense outcome *tV-si,* and that sometime early in the development of Finnish, *taita-* was attracted to the *tV-si* outcome on the basis of this semantic proximity (Laalo 1988:16-17).

Accordingly, I changed the primitive data set so that the outcome of *taita-* was *tV-si* instead of the original *a-oi.* I then ran through the same procedure as before to see if this change would trigger any other changes in the primitive data set. In the first run through the eighteen verbs, *lähte-* was once more changed from *hte-ksi* to *V-i,* but on the next run no other verb was changed. Thus the stability of the primitive data set is not weakened by the semantic similarity of *taita-* and *tietä-*. Semantic similarity seems plausible enough as an explanation for why the historical outcome *a-oi* might be replaced by *tV-si* in this one verb, but it cannot explain the overall tendency for verbs of the form -V^1([resonant])*tÆ#* to switch from *tV-si* to *V-i.* In fact, the emergence of *taisi* could never be used to explain such a tendency: the innovative *taisi* is an example of the *tV-si* outcome and could only hinder the replacement of *tV-si* by *V-i.*

I finally considered the effect of a principle of homophone avoidance on the past tense forms. Many students of the Finnish language as well as ordinary Finnish speakers have suggested that in order to maintain word distinctiveness some past tense forms take the *V-i* outcome rather than the expected *tV-si* outcome. I therefore considered the following rule of homophone avoidance for the Finnish verb system:

> *If the expected form of the past tense merges with the past tense form of another verb, then in order to avoid ambiguity replace the expected past tense form by an alternative form (where possible).*

This rule is consistent with a general principle of homophone avoidance and can be supported by examples from historical change in other languages. Homophones generally do not cause any misunderstanding as long as the homophones manifest some "differences of grammatical function" (Bloomfield 1933:396) or are from "different subsystems of the language" (Lehmann 1962:131). But whenever we have cases of "intolerable" or "insidious" homophony (Anttila 1972:182), there is a definite tendency to remove the confusion. Historical linguists generally mention a couple of well-known examples of homophone avoidance: Gilliéron's famous example of the merger of 'rooster' and 'cat' as *gat* in southwest France and the subsequent replacement of *gat* 'rooster' by other words; and the loss of the verb *let* 'prevent' in early modern English because of its merger with the historically different verb *let* 'allow' (Bloomfield 1933:396-399). And Anttila (1972:181-182) adds a number of examples from other languages.

This well-defined rule of homophone avoidance permitted me to change the past tense of two verbs in the primitive data set from *si* to *ti: kyntä-* 'plow' and *nouta-* 'fetch'. These verbs each have two theoretically possible past tense forms:

kyntä-	*kynsi / kynti*
nouta-	*nousi / nouti*

In contrast, the two verbs *kynsi-* 'scratch' and *nouse-* 'rise' have only one possible past tense form (as described in section 1 of this chapter):

kynsi-	*kynsi*
nouse-	*nousi*

In order to avoid ambiguity, the speaker is forced to choose the *V-i* past tense for the verbs *kyntä-* 'plow' and *nouta-* 'fetch'.[7]

Sometimes a more powerful principle of homophone avoidance has been invoked for Finnish, one that disallows any past tense form that merges with any frequently occurring word form, not just another past tense form.[8] Using a more general principle of homophone avoidance, theoretically possible past tense forms like *pisi, vesi,* and *vuosi* have sometimes been disallowed because they lead to simple word mergers (but not the merging of past tense forms):[9]

pitä-	'hold'	**pisi* > *piti* (1st sg: **pisin*)	*pisin* (superlative: *pitkä* 'tall')
vetä-	'pull'	**vesi* > *veti*	*vesi* (noun: 'water')
vuota-	'leak'	**vuosi* > *vuoti*	*vuosi* (noun: 'year')

In order to test the restricted principle of homophone avoidance on the historical development of Finnish, the original *tV-si* outcome is replaced by the *V-i* outcome for only two verbs in the data set, *kyntä-* 'plow' and *nouta-* 'fetch'. We then see if this change will cause any of the other *tV-si* verbs in our primitive data set to take on the regular *V-i* outcome. To make sure that there is no help from other verbs that might take the *V-i* outcome,

---

[7] Anttila 1972:182 also gives the infrequent verb *kute-* 'spawn' as an example of this kind of homophone avoidance; in this case the competing verb is also considered vulgar, *kuse-* 'urinate'. Laalo 1988:13 adds another rare example of potential homophone avoidance: *suota-* 'ooze' versus *suosi-* 'favor'.

[8] See, for example, Whitney 1956:76-77, Saarimaa 1971:26, and Fromm 1982:57. Of course, Whitney, Saarimaa, and Fromm also give the two verbs *kyntä-* 'plow' and *nouta-* 'fetch' as examples of homophone avoidance. Interestingly, these two verbs are the only examples of homophone avoidance cited in Setälä and Sadeniemi 1972:38-39.

[9] In these reconstructed forms I have ignored other historical changes: for example, the diphthongization of long mid vowels, as in **voota-* > *vuota-* 'leak'; and irrelevant older changes such as *m* > *n* / __#, as in **pisim* > *pisin* 'tallest'.

we always keep the historical past tense form *läksi* for *lähte-* 'depart' in every data set. In addition, we allow *taita-* 'know how' to take the innovative past tense form *taisi* in every data set, thus making it all that harder for *V-i* to overcome *tV-si*. These two assumptions make sense from an historical perspective, since *läksi* still exists in dialectal Finnish, but there seems to be no evidence at all for the original *taitoi* (Itkonen 1982:61). (The high frequency of the exceptional *läksi* is undoubtedly the reason for its resistance to regularization.)

Applying our procedure to our revised primitive data set, we find that over time all the other fourteen *tV-si* verbs listed above eventually shift over to the *V-i* outcome. In the first run, *hoita-* 'tend', *kiitä-* 'speed', *kyte-* 'smolder', *pote-* 'be sick', *souta-* 'row', *vetä-* 'pull', *vuota-* 'leak', and *yltä-* 'reach' all shift to the *V-i* outcome. On the second run, *itä-* 'germinate', *jäytä-* 'gnaw', *pitä-* 'hold', and *säätä-* 'enact' switch over. On the third run *syytä-* 'toss' changes, and finally on the fourth run the last verb *sietä-* 'tolerate' takes on the regular *V-i* outcome. After one additional run, the probability of the regular *V-i* outcome is further strengthened. And when we finally allow *lähte-* 'depart' to be regularized, we end up with the predictions for modern standard Finnish.

PREDICTED BEHAVIOR

for 14 verbs of the form -V^1([resonant])*tÆ#*

primitive data set: no changes in outcome; morphological stability

revised primitive data set:

		ORIGINAL	REVISED
homophone avoidance:			
kyntä-	'plow'	*tV-si*	*V-i*
nouta-	'fetch'	*tV-si*	*V-i*
semantic similarity:			
taita-	'know how'	*a-oi*	*tV-si*

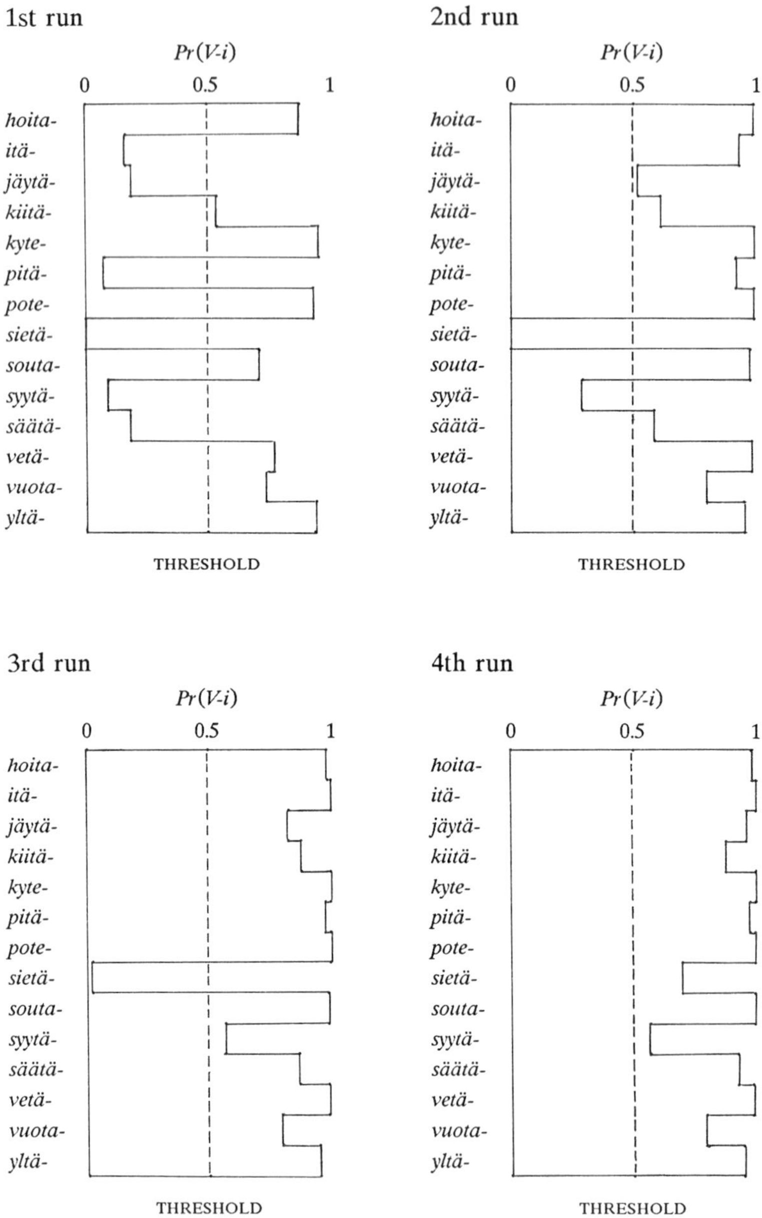
1st run
Pr(V-i)
0
0.5
1
hoita-
itä-
jäytä-
kiitä-
kyte-
pitä-
pote-
sietä-
souta-
syytä-
säätä-
vetä-
vuota-
yltä-
THRESHOLD
2nd run
Pr(V-i)
0
0.5
1
hoita-
itä-
jäytä-
kiitä-
kyte-
pitä-
pote-
sietä-
souta-
syytä-
säätä-
vetä-
vuota-
yltä-
THRESHOLD
3rd run
Pr(V-i)
0
0.5
1
hoita-
itä-
jäytä-
kiitä-
kyte-
pitä-
pote-
sietä-
souta-
syytä-
säätä-
vetä-
vuota-
yltä-
THRESHOLD
4th run
Pr(V-i)
0
0.5
1
hoita-
itä-
jäytä-
kiitä-
kyte-
pitä-
pote-
sietä-
souta-
syytä-
säätä-
vetä-
vuota-
yltä-
THRESHOLD

5th run

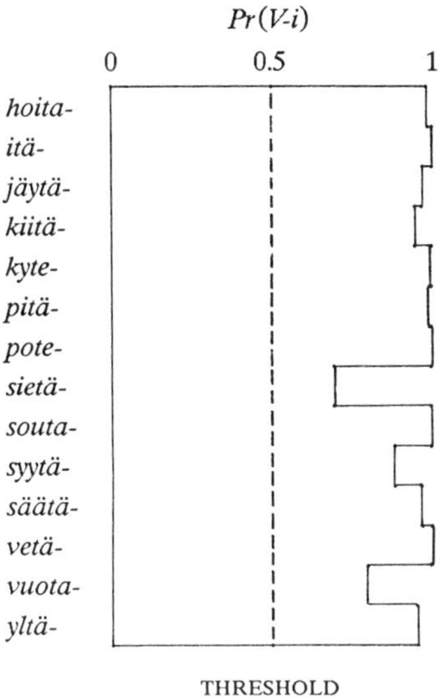

6th run

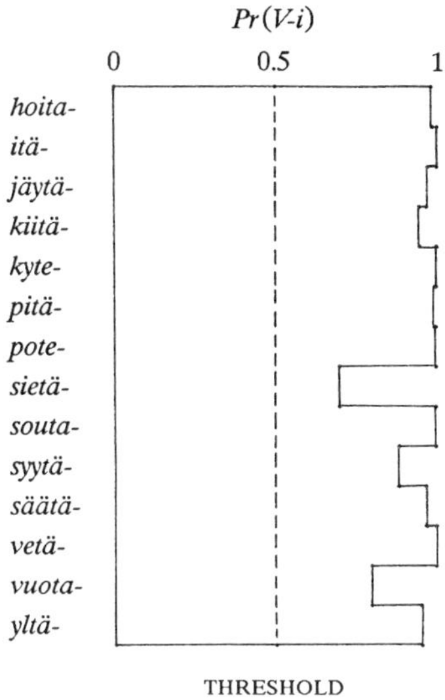

These results show that there is no need in this example for a more general definition of homophone avoidance. By the end of the second run, the three verbs *pitä-* 'hold', *vetä-* 'pull', and *vuota-* 'leak' have all taken on the regular *V-i* outcome.

The main consequence of homophone avoidance is that it breaks up a relatively weak gang effect in the context -V^1([resonant])*tÆ#*, thus permitting the strong gang effect of a large number of verbs in the nearby context -*V*[obstruent]*tA#* to attract the relatively few verbs in -*VtA#* towards the *V-i* outcome. We can see this effect when we note which verbs have the most influence in shifting the outcome of our fourteen verbs; those verbs in the nearby context -*V*[obstruent]*tA#* that take the *V-i* outcome are given in bold in the following listing:[10]

---

[10] For the meanings of the analogical words, see appendix 2.5.

RUN	VERB	STRONGEST ANALOGIES
1	*hoita-*	***koitta-, loista-, poista-, soitta-, toista-, voitta-***
	kiitä-	***kiistä-, kiittä-, keittä-***
	kyte-	*kytke-; kylpe-; koke-*
	pote-	*polke-; koke-, ole-*
	souta-	*nouta-;* ***jousta-; soitta-***
	vetä-	***estä-, kestä-, pettä-***
	vuota-	*vuole-;* ***luotta-, tuotta-***
	yltä-	*kylvä-; kylpe-, nylke-*
2	*itä-*	*ime-; iske-, itke-*
	jäytä-	***käyttä-, näyttä-, täyttä-***
	pitä-	***pistä-;*** *pote-;* ***pettä-***
	säätä-	***säästä-; päästä-, päättä-***
3	*syytä-*	***syyttä-; syöttä-;*** *syökse-*
4	*sietä-*	*syytä-, säätä-;* ***syyttä-, syöttä-, säästä-***

Finally, we might ask if there is any other way to get from the primitive data set to the modern language. For instance, could the regularization of other verbs instead of *kyntä-* 'plow' and *nouta-* 'fetch' lead to the instability of -V^1([resonant])*tÆ#*? It is true that the regularization of other verbs leads to some instability, yet these verbs do not ultimately lead to the modern language unless *kyntä-* is included as one of these regularized verbs. This is simply because the modern language cannot on the basis of phonetic similarity alone predict *kynti* rather than *kynsi.*[11] In fact, it turns out that all we need to do is regularize *kyntä-* to cause all the other fifteen verbs in the context -V^1([resonant])*tÆ#* to take on the *V-i* outcome:

RUN	0	1	2	3	4	5	6	7	8
VERBS	*kyntä-*	*kyte-*	*vetä-*	*pitä-*	*itä-*	*hoita-*	*nouta-*	*souta-*	*sietä-*
	taita-	*pote-*			*kiitä-*	*jäytä-*	*säätä-*	*syytä-*	
		yltä-				*vuota-*			

[11] See section 6 of this chapter for the synchronic discussion of *kyntä-*.

So *kyntä-* 'plow' alone is both a necessary and sufficient cause of the instability that leads to the regularization of the *V-i* outcome in the context -V^1([resonant])*tÆ#*. A restricted principle of homophone avoidance guarantees the regularization of *kyntä-* (both synchronically and diachronically) and will also include the verb *nouta-* 'fetch' as a cause of the historical drift.

Thus an analogical approach provides a viable means for understanding the tendency towards the *V-i* outcome in the historical development of Finnish, as well as the current tendencies in the standard language. In comparison, consider the complicated (and non-explicit) explanations found in Laalo 1988:10-22. Laalo explains the competition between *tV-si* and *V-i* in terms of four main principles (1-4), plus a couple of minor ones (5-6):

(1) *verb stem cohesion* (namely, the syllable structure of the verb stem):

if the stressed vowel is short (*V*) rather than long (*VV*),
V-i is favored;
if the segment preceding the *t* is a sonorant (*S*),
tV-si is favored.

These syllable constraints form a continuum of possibilities:

STEM FORM	OUTCOME
VtA# (e.g., *pitä-* 'hold')	only *V-i* is possible
VVtA# (e.g., *kiitä-* 'speed') *VStA#* (e.g., *yltä-* 'reach')	both *V-i* and *tV-si* occur
VVStA# (e.g., *piirtä-* 'draw')	*tV-si* strongly favored

(2) *homophone avoidance* (restricted version):

kyntä- 'plow': *kynti*
(not *kynsi* because of *kynsi-* 'scratch')

nouta- 'fetch': *nouti*
(not *nousi* because of *nouse-* 'rise')

suota- 'ooze': *suoti*
(not *suosi* because of *suosi-* 'favor')

(3) *dissimilation* (avoidance of *s*__*s* sequences):

souta- 'row': *souti* (not *sousi*)

syytä- 'toss': *syyti* (not *syysi*)

säätä- 'enact': *sääti* (not *sääsi*)

(4) *analogy to individual forms:*

siirtä- 'move': *siirsi*
(rather than the dissimilated *siirti*)

The past tense form *siirsi* is due to the analogical influence of a single verb, *piirtä-* 'draw': *piirsi.*

(5) *backness of stressed vowel:*

sorta- 'oppress': *sorti*

Back vowels favor the *V-i* outcome.

(6) *frequency:*

Highly frequent forms can override the above principles and retain their historical outcome.

We make a few observations about Laalo's approach. First, the term analogy is only used to refer to the influence of specific words close to a given word (for example, *siirtä-* 'move' takes *siirsi* because of a single word, *piirtä-* 'draw'). On the other hand, when the outcome is affected by individual segment types (such as the length and backness of the stressed vowel or the occurrence of a sonorant after the vowel), Laalo refers to rule-like tendencies rather than extending the notion of analogy to account for similarly-behaving clusters of words. Of course, this distinction between idiosyncratic analogy and rule-governed behavior is characteristic of all work in linguistics. Unlike the traditional linguistic distinction between analogy and rules, the analogical approach of this book makes no inherent distinction between analogy due to the influence of a single word (traditional analogy) and analogy due to the gang effect of similarly behaving words (traditional rules). In addition, there is no need to appeal to dissimilation in order to explain why *souta-* 'row', *syytä-* 'toss', and *säätä-* 'enact' take *V-i* rather than *tV-si*. The analogical approach explicitly predicts that each of these verbs will strongly favor the *V-i* outcome (see section 6). Of course, both approaches do refer to homophone avoidance and the frequency of word forms, but the analogical approach of this book proposes that homophone avoidance in a couple verbs (*kyntä-* and *nouta-*) sharply reduced the gang effect in a class of *tV-si* verbs, thus leading to the historical replacement of *tV-si* by *V-i* for all but a few frequent verbs in this class. Laalo, on the other hand, uses homophone avoidance to explain only the specific past tense forms for three verbs (*kyntä-*, *nouta-*, and *suota-*).

8. A Note on the Historical Development

PAUL Kiparsky (1973), in opposition to all previous (and subsequent) work in Finnish historical linguistics (Posti 1953:53; Hakulinen 1979:43-44,53; Rapola 1966:235-238; Häkkinen 1985:23-24,59), has claimed that sequences of [resonant]*tÆi* did not originally undergo palatalization (*t* > *t́ś* / __ *i*). The reason for this, according to Kiparsky, is that vowel simplification (*Æi* > *i*) occurred after palatalization. For the verbs under discussion this proposal predicts that the past tense forms ending in *ti* are all original while the *si* forms are due to later developments; that is, the past tense forms for *pitä-* 'hold', *tunte-* 'feel', *piirtä-* 'draw', *rakenta-* 'build', *tietä-* 'know', *pyytä-* 'request', and so forth all originally ended in *ti,* not *si.* The source for the innovative past tense forms ending in *si* are, in Kiparsky's view, from verbs like *haluta* 'want' which have past tense forms ending in *si: halua-* ~ *halusi.* He claims that *halusi* is historically derived from **halut* + *i* and thus palatalization applied. The assumption underlying this reconstruction is that this word (and others like it) had an historically independent consonant stem, *halut,* in addition to a vowel stem, *haluta.* Kiparsky argues for this on the basis of the past participle form *halunnut,* which he claims comes from **halut* + *nut.* Actually, there is no need to reconstruct any historically independent consonant stems for verbs like *haluta.* Historically these verbs are morphologically derived by adding a verbalizing suffix *tA* to nouns like *halu* 'desire', which means that the consonant stem is derived from the vowel stem. Thus *halunnut* is ultimately derived from **haluta* + *nut* by vowel loss and assimilation while *halusi* is ultimately derived from **haluta* + *i* by vowel simplification and palatalization. As evidence for these reconstructions, I would cite the parallel historical development for a verb like *tietä-* 'know' with its past participle form *tiennyt* (~ *tietänyt*) and its past tense form *tiesi*.

Kiparsky also chooses to ignore crucial examples of *tÆi* > *si:* for example, there are plural nominal stems such as *käsi-* 'hands' (< **käte* + *i*) and *tuhansi-* 'thousands' (< **tuhante* + *i*). Of special value as evidence is an old dialectal form of *kunta-* 'area of local authority or government': namely, the instrumental form *-kunsin* (as in *kirkkokunsin* 'by church parishes' – see Hakulinen 1979:44). This form is historically derived from **kunta* + *i* + *n*. Generally, plural stems derived from *-tA* + *i* have been analogically leveled: thus the historical plural stem **sosi-* 'wars' (derived from **sota* + *i*) has been replaced by *soti-*. In the same way, the normal plural stem of *kunta-* is now *kunti-*.

Another problem with Kiparsky's analysis is that it cannot explain why the supposed analogical replacement of *ti* by *si* has affected only the most frequent verbs in the $-V^1VtA\#$ category (*tietä-* 'know', *pyytä-* 'request', *löytä-* 'find', and *huuta-* 'shout'), but not the less frequent verbs (*jouta-* 'have time', *hoita-* 'tend', *jäätä-* 'freeze', *jäytä-* 'gnaw', *suota-* 'ooze', *nouta-* 'fetch', and so on).[12]

[12] For a more extensive evaluation of Kiparsky's proposal, see Laalo 1988:30-35.

Chapter Six

CONCLUSION

1. Massively Parallel Processing of Analogical Sets

IN section 3.1 we noted that there are 2^n supracontexts for n variables. Using sequential processing, this requires an exponential running time on the order of 2^n. We can reduce the running time to a simple function of n if we use massively parallel processing (as described in Hillis 1985).

In order to see the advantages of parallel over sequential processing, consider the following network of $2^n = 16$ supracontexts for a given context of $n = 4$ variables:

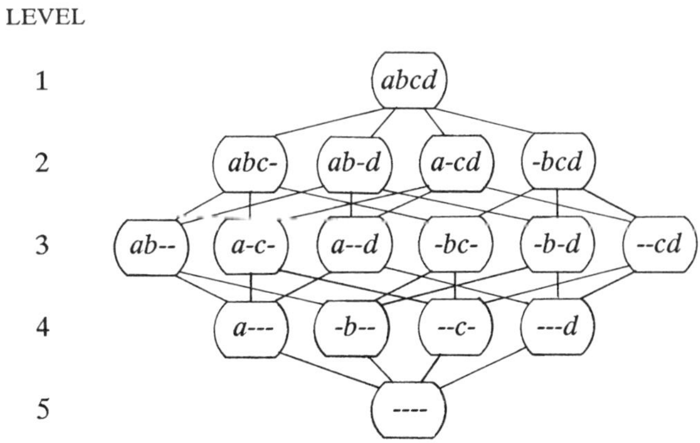

Sequential processing forces us to determine the heterogeneity of each supracontext one at a time, which leads to the exponential running time on the order of 2^n. We start at the highest level (with the given context *abcd*) and move systematically through the network, a level at a time, determining the heterogeneity of each supracontext in order.

Alternatively, suppose we place a processor at each supracontextual node in the network so that the heterogeneity of each supracontext can be determined at any time instead of sequentially. We would again start at the highest level, with the most specific supracontext (namely, the given context *abcd*). After determining the heterogeneity of the given context, we would send this information to the four nodes of the second level. We would then determine the heterogeneity for each of the supracontexts at the second level. Because there is a separate processor at each node, it would only take one processing cycle to determine the heterogeneity for all the supracontexts on the second level. This information would then be sent along the appropriate paths to the six supracontexts on the third level. And then the heterogeneity for all the supracontexts on the third level could be determined within a single processing cycle. And so on until the heterogeneity of the unspecified supracontext (----) on the fifth (or lowest) level would be determined. Each level of the network would require a single processing cycle. In all, there will be $n + 1$ levels in a network of supracontexts since each succeeding level represents the removal of one additional variable. By placing a processor at each node in the network, each level requires one processing cycle. Thus massively parallel processing reduces the processing time for determining the analogical set to a simple function of the number of variables.

Actually, the hardware requirements can also be reduced using massively parallel processing, but not as dramatically as the running time. In the above example (which involved four variables), we placed a processor at each node of the network, yet we determined heterogeneity at only one level at a time. While determining the heterogeneity at a given level, all the other processors at the other levels were idle. Since the level with the most nodes (the third one) contains only six supracontexts, we actually need only six parallel processors to reduce the running time to a function of the number of variables. This is a considerable savings in hardware (from sixteen processors to six).

In general, given n variables, we need only enough parallel processors to handle the level with the most nodes. For large n this maximal number of processors is approximately equal to $(\sqrt{2/\pi n})2^n$. Using parallel processing we can therefore reduce the hardware requirements by a factor on the order of $1/\sqrt{n}$.

2. A Final Analogy

DESPITE the many arguments, both empirical and conceptual, in favor of an analogical approach to the description of language, there is a place for rule approaches too. An optimal rule description serves as a kind of metalanguage that efficiently describes past behavior and allows us to talk about that behavior. Whenever we attempt to summarize behavior or to discover relationships in data, our viewpoint is structuralist. But if we wish to predict language behavior rather than just describe it, we must abandon rule approaches. Rule descriptions have great difficulty in explaining actual language usage.

A comparable situation exists in the field of physics. Long before the atomic model of gases was developed, various laws were discovered about the properties of gases (Holton and Roller 1958:366-371):

> *Boyle's Law:* the pressure of a gas is inversely proportional to the volume of the gas (assuming the temperature is kept constant);
>
> *Charles' (and Gay-Lussac's) Law:* the volume of a gas is directly proportional to the absolute temperature of the gas (assuming the pressure is kept constant).

In actual fact, these laws only approximate the real behavior of gases. For instance, for pressures greater than ten atmospheres or for certain gases such as water vapor and carbon dioxide near liquefaction, Boyle's law is not very accurate (Holton and Roller 1958:457).

It is obvious that these gas laws cannot be viewed as fundamental. Instead, these relationships are derived from the general kinetic properties of individual gas molecules acting in an aggregate.[1] A gas may appear to be following Boyle's and Charles' laws, yet in actuality these laws have no existence except in the minds of scientists. Such laws are meta-descriptive devices that scientists use to talk about the properties of gases. In no literal sense can it be said that individual gas molecules follow these laws.

In a similar way, linguistic rules are meta-descriptive devices that exist only in the minds of linguists. Speakers do not appear to use rules in perceiving and producing language. Moreover, linguistic rules can only explain language behavior for ideal situations. As in physics, an atomistic approach seems to be a more promising method for predicting language behavior.

---

[1] For an excellent description of how the atomistic model of gases accounts for these laws, see chapter 4 of Reif 1967.

REFERENCES

Anttila, Raimo (1972). *An Introduction to Historical and Comparative Linguistics* (New York: Macmillan).

Bloom, Lois, Patsy Lightbown, and Lois Hood (1975). *Structure and Variation in Child Language,* Monographs of the Society for Research in Child Development, volume 40, number 2.

Bloomfield, Leonard (1933). *Language* (New York: Holt, Rinehart and Winston).

Cedergren, Henrietta J. and David Sankoff (1974). "Variable Rules: Performance as a Statistical Reflection of Competence", *Language* 50:333-355.

Chomsky, Noam (1965). *Aspects of the Theory of Syntax* (Cambridge, Massachusetts: MIT Press).

Derwing, Bruce L. (1979). "English Pluralization: A Testing Ground for Rule Evaluation", *Experimental Linguistics: Integration of Theories and Applications,* edited by Gary D. Pridcaux, Bruce L. Derwing, and William J. Baker (Ghent, Belgium: E. Story-Scientia), 81-112.

Derwing, Bruce L. and Terrance M. Nearey (1986). "Experimental Phonology at the University of Alberta", *Experimental Phonology,* edited by John J. Ohala and Jeri J. Jaeger (Orlando, Florida: Academic Press), 187-209.

Fasold, Ralph W. (1978). "Language Variation and Linguistic Competence", *Linguistic Variation: Models and Methods,* edited by David Sankoff (New York: Academic Press), 85-95.

Finnish Research Center for Domestic Languages, statistical analysis of approximately 610,000 words of text from twenty-six issues of *Suomen Kuvalehti* [1975:36 through 1976:11] (available on microfiche).

Fletcher, Paul (1985). *A Child's Learning of English* (Oxford: Basil Blackwell).

Francis, W. Nelson and Henry Kučera, with the assistance of Andrew W. Mackie (1982). *Frequency Analysis of English Usage: Lexicon and Grammar* (Boston: Houghton Mifflin).

Fromkin, Victoria A. (1971). "The Non-Anomalous Nature of Anomalous Utterances", *Language* 47:27-52.

Fromm, Hans (1982). *Finnische Grammatik* (Heidelberg: Carl Winter).

Gates, Arthur I. (1937). *A List of Spelling Difficulties in 3876 Words* (New York: Teachers College, Columbia University).

Grant, David A., Harold W. Hake, and John P. Hornseth (1951). "Acquisition and Extinction of a Verbal Conditioned Response with Differing Percentages of Reinforcement", *Journal of Experimental Psychology* 42 (July):1-5.

Guy, Gregory R. (1980). "Variation in the Group and the Individual: The Case of Final Stop Deletion", *Locating Language in Time and Space,* edited by William Labov (New York: Academic Press), 1-54.

Hakulinen, Lauri (1979). *Suomen kielen rakenne ja kehitys,* 4th edition (Helsinki: Otava).

Häkkinen, Kaisa (1985). *Suomen kielen äänne- ja muotorakenteen historiallista taustaa,* volume 6 of *Fennistica* (Turku: Åbo Akademi, Suomen kielen laitos).

Hays, William L. (1973). *Statistics for the Social Sciences,* 2nd edition (New York: Holt, Rinehart and Winston).

Hillis, W. Daniel (1985). *The Connection Machine* (Cambridge, Massachusetts: MIT Press).

Holton, Gerald and Duane H. D. Roller (1958). *Foundations of Modern Physical Science* (Reading, Massachusetts: Addison-Wesley).

Itkonen, Terho (1982). *Kieliopas* (Helsinki: Kirjayhtymä).

Jacobs, Roderick A. and Peter S. Rosenbaum (1968). *English Transformational Grammar* (Waltham, Massachusetts: Blaisdell).

Johnson, Dale D. and Richard L. Venezky (1976). "Models for Predicting How Adults Pronounce Vowel Digraph Spellings in Unfamiliar Words", *Visible Language* 10:257-268.

Karlsson, Fred (1982). *Suomen kielen äänne- ja muotorakenne* (Porvoo: Werner Söderström).

Kiparsky, Paul (1973). "Productivity in Phonology", *Issues in Phonological Theory: Proceedings of the Urbana Conference on Phonology,* edited by Michael J. Kenstowicz and Charles W. Kisseberth (The Hague: Mouton), 169-176.

Laalo, Klaus (1988). *Imperfektimuotojen* ti~si-*vaihtelu suomen kielessä* (Helsinki: Suomalaisen Kirjallisuuden Seura).

Labov, William (1970). "The Study of Language in its Social Context", *Studium Generale* 23:30-87.

Labov, William (1973). "The Boundaries of Words and Their Meanings", *New Ways of Analyzing Variation in English,* edited by Charles-James N. Bailey and Roger W. Shuy (Washington, D.C.: Georgetown University Press), 340-373.

Lehiste, Ilse (1970). *Suprasegmentals* (Cambridge, Massachusetts: MIT Press).

Lehmann, Winfred P. (1962). *Historical Linguistics: an Introduction* (New York: Holt, Rinehart and Winston).

Lisker, Leigh and Arthur S. Abramson (1964). "A Cross-Language Study of Voicing in Initial Stops: Acoustical Measurements", *Word* 20:384-422.

Lisker, Leigh and Arthur S. Abramson (1970). "The Voicing Dimension: Some Experiments in Comparative Phonetics", *Proceedings of the Sixth International Congress of Phonetic Sciences, Held at Prague 7-13 September 1967,* edited by Bohuslav Hála, Milan Romportl, and Přemysl Janota (Prague: Czechoslovak Academy of Sciences), 563-567.

McClelland, James L. and David E. Rumelhart (1980). "An Interactive Activation Model of the Effect of Context in Perception", CHIP 91 (part I) and CHIP 95 (part II) (La Jolla, California: Center for Human Information Processing, University of California at San Diego).

Messick, Samuel J. and Charles M. Solley (1957). "Probability Learning in Children: Some Exploratory Studies", *The Journal of Genetic Psychology* 90:23-32.

Nykysuomen sanakirja (*NSSK*), edited by Matti Sadeniemi (Porvoo: Werner Söderström, 1973).

Paunonen, Heikki (1973). "On Free Variation", *Suomalais-ugrilaisen Seuran Aikakauskirja* 72:285-300.

Posti, Lauri (1953). "From Pre-Finnic to Late Proto-Finnic", *Finnisch-Ugrische Forschungen* 31:1-91.

Rapola, Martti (1966). *Suomen kielen äännehistorian luennot* (Helsinki: Suomalaisen Kirjallisuuden Seura).

Reif, Frederick (1967). *Statistical Physics,* Berkeley Physics Course, volume 5 (New York: McGraw-Hill).

Rousseau, Pascale and David Sankoff (1978). "Advances in Variable Rule Methodology", *Linguistic Variation: Models and Methods,* edited by David Sankoff (New York: Academic Press), 57-95.

Rumelhart, David E. (1979). "Analogical Processes and Procedural Representations", CHIP 81 (La Jolla, California: Center for Human Information Processing, University of California at San Diego).

Rumelhart, David E. and James L. McClelland (1985). "On Learning the Past Tenses of English Verbs", ICS Report 8507 (La Jolla, California: Institute for Cognitive Science, University of California at San Diego). [This also appears in Rumelhart, McClelland, and the PDP Research Group 1986, volume II:216-271.]

Rumelhart, David E. and James L. McClelland, and the PDP Research Group (1986). *Parallel Distributed Processing: Explorations in the Microstructure of Cognition,* 2 volumes (Cambridge, Massachusetts: MIT Press).

Saarimaa, E. A. (1971). *Kielenopas* (Porvoo: Werner Söderström).

Saukkonen, Pauli, Marjatta Haipus, Antero Niemikorpi, and Helena Sulkala (1979). *Suomen kielen taajuussanasto* (Porvoo: Werner Söderström).

Saussure, Ferdinand de (1966). *Course in General Linguistics,* edited by Charles Bally and Albert Sechehaye, translated by Wade Baskin (New York: McGraw-Hill).

Scragg, D. G. (1974). *A History of English Spelling* (Manchester, England: Manchester University Press).

Setälä, E. N. and Matti Sadeniemi (1972). *Suomen kielioppi: Äänne- ja sanaoppi* (Helsinki: Otava).

Skousen, Royal (1979). "Empirical Interpretations of Psychological Reality", *Proceedings of the Ninth International Congress of Phonetic Sciences,* volume II, edited by Eli Fischer-Jørgensen, Jørgen Rischel, and Nina Thorsen (Copenhagen: Institute of Phonetics, University of Copenhagen), 121-128.

Skousen, Royal (1983). *Analogy and Structure* (unpublished 480-page manuscript).

Skousen, Royal (1986). "Through a Glass Darkly: Trying to Understand the Scriptures", *BYU Studies* 26 (Fall):3-20.

Webster's Ninth New Collegiate Dictionary (Springfield, Massachusetts: Merriam-Webster, 1983).

Whitney, Arthur H. (1956). *Teach Yourself Finnish* (London: English Universities Press).

Winograd, Terry (1975). "Frame Representations and the Declarative/ Procedural Controversy", *Representation and Understanding: Studies in Cognitive Science,* edited by Daniel G. Bobrow and Allan Collins (New York: Academic Press), 185-210.

Appendix One

SYMBOLS FOR THE PHONEMES OF ENGLISH

THE following linguistic symbols are used in the text of the book, the digraph symbols are used in appendix 2.2, and the single-byte symbols are used for computer representations of variables.

	LINGUISTIC	DIGRAPH	SINGLE-BYTE
pore	p	p	p
berry	b	b	b
tin	t	t	t
dumb	d	d	d
cat	k	k	k
gun	g	g	g
chin	č	c	c
jaw	ǰ	j	j

fun	f	f	f
very	v	v	v
thin	θ	T	T
the	ð	D	D
see	s	s	s
zoo	z	z	z
shoe	š	S	S
azure	ž	Z	Z
hot	h	h	h
money	m	m	m
nuts	n	n	n
sing	ŋ	N	N
lawn	l	l	l
rob	r	r	r
win	w	w	w
while	hw	hw	W
yes	y	y	y
beat	i	i	i
bit	ɪ	I	I
bait	ei	ei	$
bet	ɛ	e	e
bat	æ	a	a
boot	u	u	u
put	ʊ	U	U
boat	ou	ou	%

caught	ɔ	o	o
cot	ɑ	A	A
by	ai	ai	!
bout	au	au	@
boy	ɔi	oi	#
murder	ɚ	*	*
above	ə	E	E

Stress marks come after the vowel:

primary stress	V^1	or	V′
secondary stress	V_2	or	V″

Appendix Two

DATA SETS

1. The Indefinite Article in English

outcomes: *a, an*

variables:

1-4 the last two phonemes in the immediately preceding word plus the syllabic representations (Consonant or Vowel) for these two phonemes

5 the type of boundary preceding the indefinite article: a phrasal break (|) or continuous (+)

6-15 the first five phonemes in the immediately following word plus the syllabic representations for these five phonemes

data set (outcome, variables, context):

```
a   CrVu+CgClVaCsØ=  through a glass darkly
a   VACs+CmV%CsCtØ=  across a most interesting book
a   VeCt+CkVACpViØ=  get a copy
a   CnCt|CfCyVuØ===  print. a few years
an  VoCr+VICnCsCtVE  for an institute class
```

an	VeCt+V*CrClViØ=	get an early version
a	VaCd+CbV@CnCdØ=	had a bound copy
a	VECv+CbVUCkØ===	of a book
an	V$Cd+VICmCpVoCr	played an important part
a	VeCn|CgCrV$CtØ=	then, a great honor
a	CkCs|CsVECbCjVI	linguistics – a subject
a	VICv+CtVoCkØ===	give a talk
a	VACn+CgVACsCpVE	on a gospel subject
a	VECm+ClVICNCgCw	from a linguistic point
a	VICv+CtVoCkØ===	give a talk
a	V@Ct+CnVECmCbV*	about a number
a	VaCz+CfV*CrCsCt	as a first example
a	ClVi+ClVICtV*Cr	occasionally a literary use
a	VaCv+CfCyVuØ===	have a few relics
an	VoCr+V@CtChV@Cs	for an outhouse
a	CsV%+CyVuCfVECm	also a euphemism
an	CnCd+VoCrCdVECn	and an ordinary reader
a	VaCz+CfV!CnVECl	as a final example
a	VICn+CmV$CnCjV*	in a manger
a	ClVi|CmV$CnCjV*	essentially, a manger
a	VICz+CfViCdVICN	is a feeding trough
a	VACn+CvV*CrCbØ=	on a verb
a	VICn+CsCtV$CbVE	in a stable
a	ViCn+CpClV$CsØ=	between a place
a	ClCz|CsCtV$CbVE	animals – a stable
a	CnCd+CpClV$CsØ=	and a place
an	V!Ct|VICnØ=====	night – an inn
a	VICn+CsCtV$CbVE	in a stable
a	VICn+CsCtV$CbVE	in a stable
an	CtVu+VICgCzVaCm	to an example
an	CdCz+VICnCkCrVi	afterwards an increase
a	VECn+CwV*CrCdØ=	often a word
a	VECv+CwVUCmVECn	of a woman's virtue
an	CcVu|VeCtVECmVE	virtue, an etymological impossibility

a	VICz+CfVUCtCnV%	is a footnote
an	CtVu+VICnCtCrVE	to an interesting comment
a	VeCm+CbClVeCsVI	them a blessing
a	CnCd+CmVaCnØ===	and a man
a	VICN+CwVoCkØ===	meaning a walk-in enclosure
an	CtVu+VICnV*CrØ=	to an inner or private room
a	VICn+ChV@CsØ===	in a house
a	VoCr+ChV@CsØ===	for a house
a	V!Cz+ClVACrCjØ=	implies a large imposing residence
an	CnCs|VACbCvViVE	residence, an obvious reward
a	CnCz+CpClV$CsØ=	means a place
a	ClVi+CdCwVeClVI	simply a dwelling place
a	VICn+ClVACrCjØ=	in a large house
a	VACt+CrVeCfV*Cr	not a reference
a	VICz+CmVoCrØ===	is a more general reference
a	VICz+CpClV*CrVE	is a plural form
a	CtVu+CkVECpVECl	to a couple
a	VECn|CrViCdV*Cr	edition. a reader
a	CtCs+CyVuCsØ===	quotes a use
a	VICN|CsVICmVECl	meaning. a similar difficulty
a	V@Ct+CkVACmVEØ=	without a comma
a	VaCz+CyVuCTØ===	as a youth
a	VECz+CmVICsCtV$	was a mistake
a	CtVu+CmVICsVECn	to a misunderstanding
a	VaCz+CkVaCrViVI	as a carrying across
a	VICn+CpVaCrVECl	in a parallel column
a	VECv+CtVeCkCsØ=	of a text
a	ClVi+CtCrVaCnCs	really a translation
an	VECz+VECtVeCmCp	was an attempt
a	ClVi|CmVICsCpCr	correctly. a misprint
a	CtVu+CdVICfV*Cr	to a different sort
a	VaCt+CnVaCtØ===	at a gnat
a	ClV%+CkVaCmVECl	swallow a camel
a	VaCt+CnVaCtØ===	at a gnat

a	VaCt+CnVaCtØ===	at a gnat
a	VICz+CpCrVICnCt	is a printing error
a	V@Ct+CnVaCtØ===	out a gnat
a	ClV%+CkVaCmVECl	swallow a camel
a	V$Ct+ClVICtVECl	tolerate a little gnat
a	VECt+CkVaCmVECl	but a camel
a	V*Cr+CkVECpVECl	consider a couple
a	CtVu+CwVoCcCmVE	to a watchman
a	VECn|CgVACrCdØ=	watchman, a guard
a	VeCt+CbVeCtV*Cr	get a better feel
a	VICz+CvVeCrViØ=	is a very literal translation
a	VICz+CkVaCrVECk	is a characteristic pose
a	VECn|CsCpVICrVE	heaven, a spiritual reward
an	V*Cr+VICgCzVaCm	consider an example
an	VeCr+VoClCtV*Cr	where an alternative translation
a	CnCz+CmVeCsVECn	means a messenger
a	CtVu+ChCyVuCmVE	to a human messenger
a	VaCn|CsVuCpV*Cr	man; a supernatural messenger
a	VACd|CgVACrCdVi	god; a guardian angel
an	VoCr+ViCvVEClØ=	or an evil spirit
a	VICn+ClVACtØ===	been a lot
a	VaCk+CmVeCsVICj	back a message
an	CvCz+VICnCkV*Cr	gives an incorrect translation
a	VECz+CrVICkClV!	was a reclining one
a	VICT+CkVUCSVECn	with a cushion
a	VICz+CTVICrViØ=	is a theory
a	VECc+CtCrVaCnCs	such a translation
an	V*Cr|ViCvVECnØ=	shoulder. an even more difficult situation
a	ClCd|CwVUCmVECn	behold, a woman
a	VECz+CsVICnV*Cr	was a sinner
an	VoCt+VaClVECbVa	brought an alabaster box
a	VICn+CcVeCrØ===	in a chair
a	VICn+CnViClVICN	in a kneeling position

a	VECv+CmVICsCtCr	of a mistranslation
a	VaCz+CfVUCtCnV%	has a footnote
a	VICn+CmVACrCvVE	in a marvelous work
a	CnCd+CwVECnCdV*	and a wonder
a	ClCd+CsVaCbVECT	called a sabbath
a	ClCd+CsVaCbVECT	called a sabbath
a	VACt+CsVaCbVECT	not a sabbath
a	VICz+CsVeCpV*Cr	is a separate word
a	VICz+CmVoCrØ===	is a more serious objection
a	VECv+CwV*CrCdØ=	of a word
a	CtVu+CpVICrViVE	to a period
a	VECv+CfVaCsCtØ=	of a fast
a	VICz+CvVeCrViØ=	is a very good reason
a	VECv+CsVeCvVECn	of a seven-day period
a	CtVu+CpVICrViVE	to a period
a	CtVu+CwViCkØ===	to a week
a	VACt+CsVECbCsCt	not a substitute
a	VoCr+CdV$Ø=====	nor a day
a	VaCz+CkCrVICsCc	as a christian sabbath
a	CtVu+CmVICsCtCr	to a mistranslation
a	CzCd+CgVUCdØ===	caused a good deal
a	VICz+CdVICsCtVI	is a distinction
a	CkCt+CbVICtØ===	detect a bit
a	VECv+CmVICsCtCr	of a mistranslation
a	CmCd+CsV*CrCtVE	performed a certain number
an	VECm+VICsCtVoCr	from an historical point
a	VECc+CkV$CsØ===	such a case
a	CmCz|CvVeCrViØ=	times, a very strange expression
an	CtCs+VECtVeCmCp	represents an attempt
a	CsV%+CkClVICrØ=	also a clear biblical allusion
a	VaCv+CdVeCfVECn	have a definite case
a	CrCv+CmVACrCjVE	deserve a marginal reading
a	VECc+ChVaCnCdVi	such a handy admonition
a	ViCn+CsCpVICrVE	seen a spirit

an	VICT+V%CpVECnØ=	with an open heart
a	VECv+ClVICNCgCw	of a linguistic study
an	VECc+VECpCrV%Cc	such an approach
a	VACt+CpVaCnVECs	not a panacea
an	V%Cn|VICnCsCpV!	alone. an inspired reading
a	VeCs|ClVICNCgCw	nevertheless, a linguistic approach
an	ClVi|VECpCrV%Cc	ultimately, an approach
a	V$Cn+CpV*CrCfVI	obtain a perfect knowledge
a	VECt+CdVICmØ===	but a dim reflection
a	VACt|ClVeCkCsVE	scott, a lexicon
a	V*Cr|CgCrViCkØ=	danker, a greek-english lexicon
an	VoCr+VICgCzVaCm	for an example
a	VECl|ChVICsCtV*	bible: a history
an	VECn|VICnCtCrVE	revelation: an introduction
a	CnCz|CmVaCnCyVE	jevons, a manual
a	CdCz|CmVACrCvVE	richards, a marvelous work
a	CnCd+CwVECnCdV*	and a wonder
a	V*Cr|CkCrVICtVE	plummer, a critical and exegetical commentary
a	CgCz|ChViCbCrVu	briggs, a hebrew and english lexicon
a	CdV$|CbVICbClVE	day: a biblical, historical, and theological investigation
a	CvVi|ChVICsCtV*	niv: a history
a	V%Cn|CgCrVaCmV*	moulton, a grammar
a	VICz+CkCwVeCsCc	is a question
an	VICT+VICNCgClVI	with an english translation

2. *Spelling of Initial /h/ in English*

outcomes: <h>, <wh>, <j>

variables:

1 the stress pattern of the word: does the first stressed vowel occur in the first (1) or second (2) syllable?

2 the phoneme immediately preceding the first vowel (either /h/ as in *he* or /y/ as in *huge*)

3 the first vowel phoneme

4-5 the two phonemes that immediately follow the first vowel

6-7 the two phonemes that immediately precede the second vowel (or if there is no second vowel, then the last two phonemes in the word)

8 the second vowel phoneme (or if there is no second vowel, then this variable is ø)

9-10 the two phonemes that immediately follow the second vowel

11 the phoneme that immediately precedes the third vowel or, if there is no third vowel but there is a second vowel, then the last phoneme in the word

12 the third vowel phoneme (or if there is no third vowel but there is a second one, then this variable is ø)

data set (outcome, variables, spelling, pronunciation):

```
h   1hab*ab*rdda haberdashery    ha'b*rda"S*ri
wh  1habEabEt=tØ habit           ha'bEt
h   1habEabEtEtE habitable       ha'bEtEbEl
h   1habEabEtata habitat         ha'bEta"t
h   1habEabEtssØ habits          ha'bEts
h   2hEbIEbIcucu habitual        hEbI'cuEl
```

h	2hEbIEbIcucu	habitually	hEbI'cuElli
h	1hak=akØ====	hack	hak
h	1haktktØ====	hacked	hakt
h	1hakIakIN=NØ	hacking	ha'kIN
h	1haknknid=dØ	hackneyed	ha'knid
h	1had=adØ====	had	had
h	1hadEadEnttØ	hadn't	ha'dEnt
h	1haftftE==EØ	hafta	ha'ftE
h	1hag*ag*rddØ	haggard	ha'g*rd
h	1hagEagElIlI	haggling	ha'gElIN
h	1h$l=$lØ====	hail	heil
h	1h$ldldØ====	hailed	heild
h	1her=erØ====	hair	her
h	1herkrkEt=tØ	haircut	he'rkE"t
h	1herzrzØ====	hairs	herz
h	1herieri==iØ	hairy	he'ri
h	1hal=alØ====	Hal	hal
h	1h$l=$lØ====	Hale	heil
h	1haf=afØ====	half	haf
h	1hafbbrid=dØ	half-breed	ha'fbri"d
h	1hafsfsencc*	half-century	ha'fs"enc*ri
h	1hafkkl%zddØ	half-closed	ha'fklou"zd
h	1hafkfkAnccE	half-conscious	ha'fkA"ncEs
h	1hafdfdEzEzE	half-dozen	ha'fdE"zEn
h	1hafddrENkkØ	half-drunk	ha'fdrE"Nk
h	1hafffflIlddØ	half-filled	ha'ffI"ld
h	1hafhfhArttE	half-hearted	ha'fhA"rtEd
h	1haf@af@r=rØ	half-hour	ha'fau"r
h	1hafmfm!l=lØ	half-mile	ha'fmai"l
h	1hafwfw$==$Ø	half-way	ha'fwei"
h	1hafbfbak=kØ	halfback	ha'fba"k
h	1hafwfw$==$Ø	halfway	ha'fwei"
h	1hol=olØ====	hall	hol
h	1hol=olØ====	Hall	hol
h	1halEalEk=kØ	Halleck	ha'lEk

h	1holmlmArkkØ	hallmark	ho'lmA"rk
h	1holmlmArksØ	hallmarks	ho'lmA"rks
h	1hal%al%d=dØ	hallowed	ha'loud
h	1holzlzØ====	halls	holz
h	1holwlw$==$Ø	hallway	ho'lwei"
h	1h$l%$l%==%Ø	halo	hei'lou
h	1hAlzlzØ====	Hals	hAlz
h	1holtltØ====	halt	holt
h	1holtltEd=dØ	halted	ho'ltEd
h	1holtltIN=NØ	halting	ho'ltIN
h	1holtltINlli	haltingly	ho'ltINli
h	1havzvzØ====	halves	havz
h	1ham=amØ====	ham	ham
h	1ham=amØ====	Ham	ham
h	1hambmb*rgg*	hamburger	ha'mb*"rg*r
h	1hambmb*rgg*	hamburgers	ha'mb*"rg*rz
h	1hamEamElttE	Hamilton	ha'mEltEn
h	1hamlmlEt=tØ	Hamlet	ha'mlEt
h	1hamlmlEt=tØ	hamlet	ha'mlEt
h	1ham=amØ====	Hamm	ham
h	1ham*am*rSS%	Hammarskjold	ha'm*rSou"ld
h	1ham*am*rSS%	Hammarskjold's	ha'm*rSou"ldz
h	1ham*am*r=rØ	hammer	ha'm*r
h	1ham*am*rddØ	hammered	ha'm*rd
h	1hamEamEt=tØ	Hammett	ha'mEt
h	1hamEamEnddØ	Hammond	ha'mEnd
h	1hampmp*r=rØ	hamper	ha'mp*r
h	1hampmp*rddØ	hampered	ha'mp*rd
h	1hamppS*r=rØ	Hampshire	ha'mpS*r
h	1hampptEn=nØ	Hampton	ha'mptEn
h	1handndØ====	hand	hand
h	1handndØ====	Hand	hand
h	1handndInglE	hand-in-glove	ha'ndI"nglE'v
h	1handdtuhaha	hand-to-hand	ha'ndtu"ha'nd
h	1handdw%vEvE	hand-woven	ha'ndwou"vEn

h	1handdbag=gØ	handbag	ha'ndba"g
h	1handdbUk=kØ	handbook	ha'ndbU"k
h	1handklasppØ	handclasp	ha'ndkla"sp
h	1handdkEfssØ	handcuffs	ha'ndkE"fs
h	1handndEd=dØ	handed	ha'ndEd
h	1handdfEl=lØ	handful	ha'ndfE"l
h	1handndikaka	handicap	ha'ndika"p
h	1handndikaka	handicapped	ha'ndika"pt
h	1handndIN=NØ	handing	ha'ndIN
h	1haNkNk*rccI	handkerchief	ha'Nk*rcI"f
h	1handndEl=lØ	handle	ha'ndEl
h	1handndElddØ	handled	ha'ndEld
h	1handndElzzØ	handles	ha'ndElz
h	1handndElIlI	handling	ha'ndElIN
h	1handdm$d=dØ	handmade	ha'ndmei'd
h	1handdzØ====	hands	handz
h	1hansnsEm=mØ	handsome	ha'nsEm
h	1hansnsEm*m*	handsomer	ha'nsEm*r
h	1handdr!tItI	handwriting	ha'ndrai"tIN
h	1handndi==iØ	handy	ha'ndi
h	1handndimama	handyman	ha'ndima"n
h	1haN=aNØ====	hang	haN
h	1haN*aN*r=rØ	hangar	ha'N*r
h	1haNdNdØ====	hanged	haNd
h	1haNEaNEn=nØ	hangin'	ha'NEn
h	1haNIaNIN=NØ	hanging	ha'NIN
h	1haNmNmEn=nØ	hangman	ha'NmEn
h	1haN%aN%v*v*	hangover	ha'Nou"v*r
h	1haNzNzØ====	hangs	haNz
h	1haNkNkØ====	Hank	haNk
h	1han%an%v*v*	Hanover	ha'nou"v*r
h	1han%an%veve	Hanoverian	ha"nouve'riEn
h	1hanznzØ====	Hans	hanz
h	1hansnsEn=nØ	Hansen	ha'nsEn
h	1hansnsEnzzØ	Hansen's	ha'nsEnz

h	2haphphaz*z*	haphazard	hapha'z*rd
h	1haplplEs=sØ	hapless	ha'plEs
h	1hapEapEn=nØ	happen	ha'pEn
h	1hapEapEnddØ	happened	ha'pEnd
h	1hapEapEnInI	happening	ha'pEnIN
h	1hapEapEnInI	happenings	ha'pEnINz
h	1hapEapEnzzØ	happens	ha'pEnz
h	1hapEapEnsta	happenstance	ha'pEnsta"ns
h	1hapiapi*ri*	happier	ha'pi*r
h	1hapiapiEsiE	happiest	ha'piEst
h	1hapEapElili	happily	ha'pEli
h	1hapiapinEnE	happiness	ha'pinEs
h	1hapiapi==iØ	happy	ha'pi
h	2hEraEraNINI	haranguing	hEra'NIN
h	2hEraErasttØ	harassed	hEra'st
h	2hEraErasIsI	harassing	hEra'sIN
h	1hArbrb*r=rØ	harbor	hA'rb*r
h	1hArbrb*rddØ	harbored	hA'rb*rd
h	1hArbrb*rzzØ	harbors	hA'rb*rz
h	1hArkrkorttØ	Harcourt	hA'rko"rt
h	1hArdrdØ====	hard	hArd
h	1hArddb#lddØ	hard-boiled	hA'rdboi"ld
h	1hArddfot=tØ	hard-fought	hA'rdfo"t
h	1hArdrdEnddØ	hardened	hA'rdEnd
h	1hArdrd*r=rØ	harder	hA'rd*r
h	1hArdrdEsttØ	hardest	hA'rdEst
h	1hArdrdIN=NØ	Harding	hA'rdIN
h	1hArddli==iØ	hardly	hA'rdli
h	1hArddnEs=sØ	hardness	hA'rdnEs
h	1hArddSIp=pØ	hardship	hA'rdSI"p
h	1hArddSIpssØ	hardships	hA'rdSI"ps
h	1hArddwer=rØ	hardware	hA'rdwe"r
h	1hArddwIk=kØ	Hardwick	hA'rdwI"k
h	1hArdrdi==iØ	Hardy	hA'rdi
h	1hArdrdi==iØ	hardy	hA'rdi

h	1herEerEm=mØ	harem	he'rEm
h	1hArkrkØ====	hark	hArk
h	1hArlrlEm=mØ	Harlem	hA'rlEm
h	1hArmrmØ====	harm	hArm
h	1hArmmdØ====	harmed	hArmd
h	1hArmmfEl=lØ	harmful	hA'rmfEl
h	1hArmmlEs=sØ	harmless	hA'rmlEs
h	2hArmrmAnInI	harmonic	hArmA'nIk
h	1hArmrmEnini	harmonies	hA'rmEniz
h	2hArmrm%nini	harmonious	hArmou'niEs
h	1hArmrmEnini	harmony	hA'rmEni
h	1hArnrnEs=sØ	harness	hA'rnEs
h	1hArnrnEsttØ	harnessed	hA'rnEst
h	1harEarElddØ	Harold	ha'rEld
h	1hArprp*rzzØ	Harper's	hA'rp*rz
h	1hArprp*rzzØ	Harpers	hA'rp*rz
h	1hArprpIN=NØ	harping	hA'rpIN
h	1hariariEtiE	Harriet	ha'riEt
h	1harEarEmEmE	Harriman	ha'rEmEn
h	1harIarINttE	Harrington	ha'rINtEn
h	1harEarEs=sØ	Harris	ha'rEs
h	1harEarEsEsE	Harris's	ha'rEsEz
h	1harEarEsEsE	Harrison	ha'rEsEn
h	1har%ar%IN%I	harrowing	ha'rouIN
h	1hariari==iØ	Harry	ha'ri
h	1hariari==iØ	harry	ha'ri
h	1hArSrSØ====	harsh	hArS
h	1hArSSli==iØ	harshly	hA'rSli
h	1hArtrtØ====	Hart	hArt
h	1hArttf*rddØ	Hartford	hA'rtf*rd
h	1hArttmEn=nØ	Hartman	hA'rtmEn
h	1hArvrv*rddØ	Harvard	hA'rv*rd
h	1hArvrvEsttØ	harvest	hA'rvEst
h	1hArvrvEstt*	Harvester	hA'rvEst*r
h	1hArvrvEsttI	harvesting	hA'rvEstIN

h	1hArvrvEstsØ	harvests	hA′rvEsts
h	1hArvrvi==iØ	Harvey	hA′rvi
h	1has=asØ====	has	has
h	1haz=azØ====	has	haz
h	1hazEazEnttØ	hasn't	ha′zEnt
h	1h$stst Ø====	haste	heist
h	1hsEsEn=nØ	hasten	hei′sEn
h	1hsEsEnddØ	hastened	hei′sEnd
h	1hsEsEnInI	hastening	hei′sEnIN
h	1h$ststElili	hastily	hei′stEli
h	1h$ststi==iØ	hasty	hei′sti
h	1hat=atØ====	hat	hat
h	1hac=acØ====	hatch	hac
h	1hactctØ====	hatched	hact
h	1hacEacEt=tØ	hatchet	ha′cEt
h	1hacIacIN=NØ	hatching	ha′cIN
h	1h$t=$tØ====	hate	heit
h	1htEtEd=dØ	hated	hei′tEd
h	1h$tftfEl=lØ	hateful	hei′tfEl
h	1h$tstsØ====	hates	heits
h	1haT=aTØ====	hath	haT
h	1haTEaTEww	Hathaway	ha′TEwei″
h	1htItIN=NØ	hating	hei′tIN
h	1h$trtrEd=dØ	hatred	hei′trEd
h	1hatstsØ====	hats	hats
h	1hotioti==iØ	haughty	ho′ti
h	1hol=olØ====	haul	hol
h	1holdldØ====	hauled	hold
h	1holIolIN=NØ	hauling	ho′lIN
h	1holzlzØ====	hauls	holz
h	1honcncEz=zØ	haunches	ho′ncEz
h	1hontntØ====	haunt	hont
h	1hontntEd=dØ	haunted	ho′ntEd
h	1hontntIN=NØ	haunting	ho′ntIN
h	1honttsØ====	haunts	honts

h	2hEvaEvanEnE	Havana	hEva'nE
h	1haf=afØ====	have	haf
h	1hav=avØ====	have	hav
h	1hvEvEn=nØ	haven	hei'vEn
h	1havEavEnttØ	haven't	ha'vEnt
h	1h$v*$v*rErE	Haverhill	hei'v*rEl
h	1havIavIN=NØ	having	ha'vIN
h	1havEavEk=kØ	havoc	ha'vEk
h	2hEw!Ew!i=!i	Hawaii	hEwai'i
h	2hEw!Ew!En!E	Hawaiian	hEwai'En
h	1hok=okØ====	hawk	hok
h	1hok=okØ====	Hawk	hok
h	1hok*ok*r=rØ	hawker	ho'k*r
h	1hokEokEnzzØ	Hawkins	ho'kEnz
h	1hoTooTornnØ	Hawthorne	ho'To"rn
h	1h$==h$Ø====	hay	hei
h	1h!dE!dEn=nØ	Haydn	hai'dEn
h	1h$z=$zØ====	Hayes	heiz
h	1h$z=$zØ====	Hays	heiz
h	1h$ststak=kØ	haystack	hei'sta"k
h	1haz*az*rddØ	hazard	ha'z*rd
h	1haz*az*rddE	hazardous	ha'z*rdEs
h	1haz*az*rdzØ	hazards	ha'z*rdz
h	1h$z=$zØ====	haze	heiz
h	1hzEzEl=lØ	hazel	hei'zEl
h	1hazlzlEt=tØ	Hazlitt	ha'zlEt
h	1hzizi==iØ	hazy	hei'zi
h	1hi==hiØ====	he	hi
h	1hid=idØ====	he'd	hid
h	1hil=ilØ====	he'll	hil
h	1hiz=izØ====	he's	hiz
h	1hed=edØ====	head	hed
h	1hedAedAn=nØ	head-on	he'dA'n
h	1hedtdtAsIsI	head-tossing	he'dtA"sIN
h	1hededk=kØ	headache	he'dei"k

h	lhededkssØ	headaches	he'dei"ks
h	lhedEedEd=dØ	headed	he'dEd
h	lhedIedIN=NØ	heading	he'dIN
h	lhedldlanddØ	headland	he'dla"nd
h	lhedldlEs=sØ	headless	he'dlEs
h	lhedldl!tssØ	headlights	he'dlai"ts
h	lhedldl!n=nØ	headline	he'dlai"n
h	lhedldl!nzzØ	headlines	he'dlai"nz
h	lhedmdmastt*	headmaster	he'dma"st*r
h	lhedkkwortt*	headquarters	he'dkwo"rt*rz
h	lhedzdzØ====	heads	hedz
h	lhedwdwAt*t*	headwaters	he'dwA"t*rz
h	lhediedi==iØ	heady	he'di
h	lhil=ilØ====	heal	hil
h	lhildldØ====	healed	hild
h	lhil*il*r=rØ	healer	hi'l*r
h	lhilIilIN=NØ	healing	hi'lIN
h	lhelTlTØ====	health	helT
h	lhelTTfEl=lØ	healthful	he'lTfEl
h	lhelTlTi*ri*	healthier	he'lTi*r
h	lhelTlTElili	healthily	he'lTEli
h	lhelTlTi==iØ	healthy	he'lTi
h	lhip=ipØ====	heap	hip
h	lhiptptØ====	heaped	hipt
h	lhIr=IrØ====	hear	hIr
h	lh*rdrdØ====	heard	h*rd
h	lhIr*Ir*r=rØ	hearer	hI'r*r
h	lhIr*Ir*rzzØ	hearers	hI'r*rz
h	lhIrIIrIN=NØ	hearing	hI'rIN
h	lhIrIIrINzzØ	hearings	hI'rINz
h	lhIrzrzØ====	hears	hIrz
h	lhIrsrs$==$Ø	hearsay	hI'rsei"
h	lh*rsstØ====	Hearst	h*rst
h	lh*rstsØ====	Hearst's	h*rsts
h	lhArtrtØ====	heart	hArt

h	1hArttbit=tØ	heartbeat	hA'rtbi"t
h	1hArtbr$kIkI	heartbreaking	hA'rtbrei"kIN
h	1hArtrtEnInI	heartening	hA'rtEnIN
h	1hArTrTØ====	hearth	hArT
h	1hArtrtElili	heartily	hA'rtEli
h	1hArttsØ====	hearts	hArts
h	1hArtrti==iØ	hearty	hA'rti
h	1hit=itØ====	heat	hit
h	1hitEitEd=dØ	heated	hi'tEd
h	1hit*it*r=rØ	heater	hi't*r
h	1hiDEiDEn=nØ	heathen	hi'DEn
h	1heD*eD*r=rØ	heather	he'D*r
h	1hitIitIN=NØ	heating	hi'tIN
h	1hiv=ivØ====	heave	hiv
h	1hivdvdØ====	heaved	hivd
h	1hevEevEn=nØ	heaven	he'vEn
h	1hevEevEnlli	heavenly	he'vEnli
h	1hevEevEnzzØ	heavens	he'vEnz
h	1hevievi*ri*	heavier	he'vi*r
h	1hevieviEsiE	heaviest	he'viEst
h	1hevEevElili	heavily	he'vEli
h	1hevievinEnE	heaviness	he'vinEs
h	1hivIivIN=NØ	heaving	hi'vIN
h	1hevievi==iØ	heavy	he'vi
h	1hibrbru==uØ	Hebrew	hi'bru
h	1hektktIk=kØ	hectic	he'ktIk
h	1hejEejEz=zØ	hedges	he'jEz
h	1hid=idØ====	heed	hid
h	1hidldlEs=sØ	heedless	hi'dlEs
h	1hil=ilØ====	heel	hil
h	1hilzlzØ====	heels	hilz
h	1hgEgEl=lØ	Hegel	hei'gEl
h	1h!t=!tØ====	height	hait
h	1h!tE!tEnddØ	heightened	hai'tEnd
h	1h!tE!tEnInI	heightening	hai'tEnIN

h	1h!tstsØ====	heights	haits
h	1heldldØ====	held	held
h	1helEelEn=nØ	Helen	he'lEn
h	1hiliiliEmiE	helium	hi'liEm
h	1hel=elØ====	hell	hel
h	1helzlzØ====	hell's	helz
h	2hEleElenInI	Hellenic	hEle'nIk
h	1helflf!r=rØ	hellfire	he'lfai"r
h	2hel%el%==%Ø	hello	helou'
h	1helmlmØ====	helm	helm
h	1helmlmEtssØ	helmets	he'lmEts
h	1helplpØ====	help	help
h	1helpptØ====	helped	helpt
h	1helplp*r=rØ	helper	he'lp*r
h	1helppfEl=lØ	helpful	he'lpfEl
h	1helppfEllli	helpfully	he'lpfElli
h	1helplpIN=NØ	helping	he'lpIN
h	1helpplEs=sØ	helpless	he'lplEs
h	1helpplEslli	helplessly	he'lplEsli
h	1helpplEsnnE	helplessness	he'lplEsnEs
h	1helppsØ====	helps	helps
h	1hem=emØ====	hem	hem
h	1hemIemINww$	Hemingway	he'mINwei"
h	1hemEemEsffI	hemisphere	he'mEsfI"r
h	1hemdmdØ====	hemmed	hemd
h	1hem*em*rIrI	hemorrhage	he'm*rIj
h	1hempsted=dØ	Hempstead	he'mpsted
h	1hen=enØ====	hen	hen
h	1hensnsØ====	hence	hens
h	1henssforTTØ	henceforth	he'nsfo"rT
h	1henccmEn=nØ	henchmen	he'ncmEn
h	1hendnd*rssE	Henderson	he'nd*rsEn
h	1henrnrietie	Henrietta	he"nrie'tE
h	1henrnri==iØ	Henry	he'nri
h	1henrnriz=zØ	Henry's	he'nriz

h	1henznzØ====	hens	henz
h	1h*r=*rØ====	her	h*r
h	1herEerEldd∅	herald	he'rEld
h	1herEerElddE	heralded	he'rEldEd
h	1h*rbrbØ====	Herb	h*rb
h	1h*rbrb*rttØ	Herbert	h*'rb*rt
h	1h*rkkyElili	Hercules	h*'rkyEli"z
h	1h*rdrdØ====	herd	h*rd
h	1h*rdrdEd=dØ	herded	h*'rdEd
h	1h*rddzØ====	herds	h*rdz
h	1hIr=IrØ====	here	hIr
h	1hIrzrzØ====	here's	hIrz
h	1hIrEIrEb@b@	hereabouts	hI'rEbau"ts
h	1hIraIraftt*	hereafter	hI"ra'ft*r
h	1hIrbrb!==!Ø	hereby	hI'rbai"
h	2hEreEredEdE	heredity	hEre'dEti
h	1hIrIIrIn=nØ	herein	hI"rI'n
h	1hIrIIrInana	hereinafter	hI'rI"na'ft*r
h	1herEerEsisi	heresy	he'rEsi
h	1hIrtrtufofo	heretofore	hI'rtu"fo'r
h	1hIrwrwIT=TØ	herewith	hI"rwI'T
h	1herEerEtItI	heritage	he'rEtIj
h	1h*rmrmEn=nØ	Herman	h*'rmEn
h	1hIr%Ir%==%Ø	hero	hI'rou
h	1hIr%Ir%z=zØ	hero's	hI'rouz
h	1hIr%Ir%z=zØ	heroes	hI'rouz
h	2hIr%Ir%Ik%I	heroic	hIrou'Ik
h	2hIr%Ir%Ik%I	heroics	hIrou'Iks
h	1her%er%En%E	heroin	he'rouEn
h	1her%er%En%E	heroine	he'rouEn
h	1her%er%Iz%I	heroism	he'rouI"zEm
h	1her=erØ====	Herr	her
h	1herIerIk=kØ	Herrick	he'rIk
h	1herIerIN=NØ	herring	he'rIN
h	1h*rzrzØ====	hers	h*rz

h	1h*rsrselffØ	herself	h*″rse′lf
h	1hezEezEtEtE	hesitancy	he′zEtEnsi
h	1hezEezEtEtE	hesitant	he′zEtEnt
h	1hezEezEtEtE	hesitantly	he′zEtEntli
h	1hezEezEtt	hesitate	he′zEtei″t
h	1hezEezEtt	hesitated	he′zEtei″tEd
h	1hezEezEtt	hesitation	he″zEtei′SEn
h	1hesiesiEniE	Hessians	he′siEnz
h	1het*et*r%r%	heterogeneous	he″t*rouji′nyEs
h	1heksksØ====	hex	heks
h	2heksksagEgE	hexagonal	heksa′gEnEl
h	2heksksamEmE	hexameter	heksa′mEt*r
h	1h$==h$Ø====	hey	hei
h	1h$d$$d$==$Ø	heyday	hei′dei″
h	1h!drdrIk=kØ	Heydrich	hai′drIk
h	1hwUwUd=dØ	Heywood	hei′wU″d
h	1h!==h!Ø====	hi	hai
h	1h!Ewh!EwAwA	Hiawatha	hai″EwA′TE
h	1hIk*Ik*riri	hickory	hI′k*ri
h	1hId=IdØ====	hid	hId
h	1hIdEIdEn=nØ	hidden	hI′dEn
h	1h!d=!dØ====	hide	haid
h	1hIdiIdiEsiE	hideous	hI′diEs
h	1hIdiIdiEsiE	hideously	hI′diEsli
h	1h!dzdzØ====	hides	haidz
h	1h!dI!dIN=NØ	hiding	hai′dIN
h	1h!rA!rArkki	hierarchy	hai′rA″rki
h	1h!==h!Ø====	high	hai
h	1h!si!silIlI	high-ceilinged	hai′si″lINd
h	1h!de!denssE	high-density	hai′de″nsEti
h	1h!enh!en*n*	high-energy	hai′e″n*rji
h	1h!le!levEvE	high-level	hai′le″vEl
h	1h!pI!pIcttØ	high-pitched	hai′pI″ct
h	1h!p@!p@rddØ	high-powered	hai′pau″rd
h	1h!prpr!sttØ	high-priced	hai′prai″st

h	1h!prpr%titi	high-protein	hai’prou”tin
h	1h!skskul=1Ø	high-school	hai’sku”l
h	1h!s@!s@nddI	high-sounding	hai’sau”ndIN
h	1h!spspid=dØ	high-speed	hai’spi”d
h	1h!spspIrErE	high-spirited	hai’spI”rEtEd
h	1h!va!valyyu	high-value	hai’va”lyu
h	1h!bo!bol=lØ	highball	hai’bo”l
h	1h!*rh!*r=rØ	higher	hai’*r
h	1h!Esh!EsttØ	highest	hai’Est
h	1h!lE!lEnddØ	highland	hai’lEnd
h	1h!lE!lEndzØ	highlands	hai’lEndz
h	1h!l!!l!t=tØ	highlight	hai’lai”t
h	1h!l!!l!tItI	highlighting	hai’lai”tIN
h	1h!l!!l!tssØ	highlights	hai’lai”ts
h	1h!li!li==iØ	highly	hai’li
h	1h!p#!p#nttØ	highpoint	hai’poi”nt
h	1h!z=!zØ====	highs	haiz
h	1h!w$!w$==$Ø	highway	hai’wei”
h	1h!w$!w$z=zØ	highways	hai’wei”z
h	1h!ja!jak*k*	hijackers	hai’ja”k*rz
h	1h!ja!jakIkI	hijacking	hai’ja”kIN
h	1h!k=!kØ====	hike	haik
h	1h!ksksØ====	hikes	haiks
h	1h!kI!kIN=NØ	hiking	hai’kIN
h	2hEleEleriri	hilarious	hEle’riEs
h	1hIl=IlØ====	hill	hIl
h	1hIl=IlØ====	Hill	hIl
h	1hIlblbIlili	hillbilly	hI’lbI”li
h	1hIlzlzØ====	hills	hIlz
h	1hIlsls!d=dØ	hillside	hI’lsai”d
h	1hIlyly*r=rØ	Hillyer	hI’ly*r
h	1hIltltØ====	hilt	hIlt
h	1hIltltEn=nØ	Hilton	hI’ltEn
h	1hIm=ImØ====	him	hIm
h	1hImEImEll	Himalayas	hI”mElei’Ez

h	1hImsmselffØ	himself	hI"mse'lf
h	1h!ndndØ====	hind	haind
h	1hIndnd*rddØ	hindered	hI'nd*rd
h	1hIndnd*rErE	hindrances	hI'nd*rEnsEz
h	1hIndndu==uØ	Hindu	hI'ndu
h	1hIndnduIzuI	Hinduism	hI'nduI"zEm
h	1hInjnjEz=zØ	hinges	hI'njEz
h	1hIntntØ====	hint	hInt
h	1hIntntEd=dØ	hinted	hI'ntEd
h	1hIntntEn=nØ	Hinton	hI'ntEn
h	1hInttsØ====	hints	hInts
h	1hIp=IpØ====	hip	hIp
h	1hIpspsØ====	hips	hIps
h	1h!rE!rEm=mØ	Hiram	hai'rEm
h	1h!r=!rØ====	hire	hair
h	1h!rdrdØ====	hired	haird
h	1h!rI!rIN=NØ	hiring	hai'rIN
h	1hIrEIrESiSi	Hiroshima	hI"rESi'mE
h	1hIz=IzØ====	his	hIz
h	1hIststØ====	hissed	hIst
h	1hIsIIsIN=NØ	hissing	hI'sIN
h	2hIststoriri	historian	hIsto'riEn
h	2hIststoriri	historian's	hIsto'riEnz
h	2hIststoriri	historians	hIsto'riEnz
h	2hIststorIrI	historic	hIsto'rIk
h	2hIststorErE	historical	hIsto'rEkEl
h	2hIststorErE	historically	hIsto'rEkli
h	1hIstst*riri	histories	hI'st*riz
h	1hIstst*riri	history	hI'st*ri
h	1hIt=ItØ====	hit	hIt
h	1hIc=IcØ====	hitch	hIc
h	1hIckckAk=kØ	Hitchcock	hI'ckA"k
h	1hIctctØ====	hitched	hIct
h	1hIcIIcIN=NØ	hitching	hI'cIN
h	1hID*ID*r=rØ	hither	hI'D*r

h	1hID*ID*rttu	hitherto	hI'D*rtu"
h	1hItltl*r=rØ	Hitler	hI'tl*r
h	1hItltl*rzzØ	Hitler's	hI'tl*rz
h	1hItstsØ====	hits	hIts
h	1hIt*It*r=rØ	hitter	hI't*r
h	1hIt*It*rzzØ	hitters	hI't*rz
h	1hItIItIN=NØ	hitting	hI'tIN
h	1h!v=!vØ====	hive	haiv
h	1horsrsØ====	hoarse	hors
h	1horssli==iØ	hoarsely	ho'rsli
h	1hAbEAbEldd Ø	hobbled	hA'bEld
h	1hAbiAbi==iØ	hobby	hA'bi
h	1hAk=AkØ====	hoc	hAk
h	1hAjpjpAj=jØ	hodgepodge	hA'jpA"j
h	1hAjEAjEz=zØ	Hodges	hA'jEz
h	1hAfEAfE==EØ	Hoffa	hA'fE
h	1hAfmfmEn=nØ	Hoffman	hA'fmEn
h	1hAg=AgØ====	hog	hAg
h	1h%gE%gEn=nØ	Hogan	hou'gEn
h	1hAgzgzØ====	hogs	hAgz
h	1h#ststEd=dØ	hoisted	hoi'stEd
h	1h%ldldØ====	hold	hould
h	1h%ldld*r=rØ	holder	hou'ld*r
h	1h%ldld*rzzØ	holders	hou'ld*rz
h	1h%ldldIN=NØ	holding	hou'ldIN
h	1h%ldldINzzØ	holdings	hou'ldINz
h	1h%lddzØ====	holds	houldz
h	1h%ldldEp=pØ	holdup	hou'ldE"p
h	1h%l=%lØ====	hole	houl
h	1h%lzlzØ====	holes	houlz
h	1hAlEAlEdd	holiday	hA'lEdei"
h	1hAlEAlEdd	holidays	hA'lEdei"z
h	1h%li%li*ri*	holier-than-thou	hou'li*rDa"nDau'
h	1h%li%linEnE	holiness	hou'linEs
h	1hAlEAlEnddØ	Holland	hA'lEnd

h	1hAl*Al*rddØ	hollered	hA'l*rd
h	1hAl*Al*rIrI	hollering	hA'l*rIN
h	1hAl%Al%==%Ø	hollow	hA'lou
h	1hAliAliwUwU	Hollywood	hA'liwU"d
h	1hAliAliwUwU	Hollywood's	hA'liwU"dz
h	1h%lmmzØ====	Holmes	houlmz
h	1hAlEAlEkAkA	holocaust	hA'lEkA"st
h	1h%lsst*r=rØ	holster	hou'lst*r
h	1h%lsst*rddØ	holstered	hou'lst*rd
h	1h%li%li==iØ	holy	hou'li
h	1h%lyly%k=kØ	Holyoke	hou'lyou"k
h	1hAmIAmIj=jØ	homage	hA'mIj
h	1h%m=%mØ====	home	houm
h	1h%mggr%n=nØ	home-grown	hou'mgrou"n
h	1h%mlmlanddØ	homeland	hou'mla"nd
h	1h%mlmli==iØ	homely	hou'mli
h	1h%mmmm$d=dØ	homemade	hou'mmei"d
h	1h%mmmm$k*k*	homemaker	hou'mmei"k*r
h	1h%mmmm$k*k*	homemakers	hou'mmei"k*rz
h	1h%m%%m%n*n*	homeowners	hou'mou"n*rz
h	1h%m*%m*r=rØ	homer	hou'm*r
h	1h%m*%m*r=rØ	Homer	hou'm*r
h	2h%me%merIrI	Homeric	houme'rIk
h	1h%m*%m*rzzØ	homers	hou'm*rz
h	1h%mzmzØ====	homes	houmz
h	1h%mssted=dØ	homestead	hou'mste"d
h	1hAmEAmEs!s!	homicide	hA'mEsai"d
h	1h%m%%m%jEjE	homogeneity	hou"moujEnei'Eti
h	1h%m%%m%jiji	homogeneous	hou"mouji'nyEs
h	1h%m%%m%jiji	homogeneously	hou"mouji'nyEsli
h	1h%m%%m%sese	homosexual	hou"mouse'kSuEl
h	1h%na%nan=nØ	Honan	hou'na'n
h	1hEniEni==iØ	honey	hE'ni
h	1hEniEnimumu	honeymoon	hE'nimu"n
h	1hEniEnisEsE	honeysuckle	hE'nisE"kEl

h	lhAN=ANØ====	Hong	hAN
h	lhANkNkitAtA	honky-tonk	hA'NkitA"Nk
h	lhAnEAnElulu	Honolulu	hA"nElu'lu
h	lhUd=UdØ====	hood	hUd
h	lhUd=UdØ====	Hood	hUd
h	lhudldlEm=mØ	hoodlum	hu'dlEm
h	lhudldlEmzzØ	hoodlums	hu'dlEmz
h	lhUdzdzØ====	hoods	hUdz
h	lhUf=UfØ====	hoof	hUf
h	lhUfsfsØ====	hoofs	hUfs
h	lhUk=UkØ====	hook	hUk
h	lhUktktØ====	hooked	hUkt
h	lhUksksØ====	hooks	hUks
h	lhUkEUkEp=pØ	hookup	hU'kE"p
h	lhup=upØ====	hoop	hup
h	lhupspsØ====	hoops	hups
h	lhut=utØ====	Hoot	hut
h	lhut=utØ====	hoot	hut
h	lhuv*uv*r=rØ	Hoover	hu'v*r
h	lhUvzvzØ====	hooves	hUvz
h	lhAp=ApØ====	hop	hAp
h	lh%p=%pØ====	hope	houp
h	lh%p=%pØ====	Hope	houp
h	lh%ptptØ====	hoped	houpt
h	lh%pttfor=rØ	hoped-for	hou'ptfo"r
h	lh%pfpfEl=lØ	hopeful	hou'pfEl
h	lh%pfpfEllli	hopefully	hou'pfElli
h	lh%pfpfElzzØ	hopefuls	hou'pfElz
h	lh%plplEs=sØ	hopeless	hou'plEs
h	lh%plplEslli	hopelessly	hou'plEsli
h	lh%plplEsnnE	hopelessness	hou'plEsnEs
h	lh%pspsØ====	hopes	houps
h	lh%pI%pIN=NØ	hoping	hou'pIN
h	lhApkpkEnzzØ	Hopkins	hA'pkEnz
h	lhAptptØ====	hopped	hApt

h	1hAp*Ap*r=rØ	hopper	hA′p*r
h	1hApIApIN=NØ	hopping	hA′pIN
h	1horEorEs=sØ	Horace	ho′rEs
h	1hordrdØ====	horde	hord
h	1horddzØ====	hordes	hordz
h	2hEr!Er!zEzE	horizon	hErai′zEn
h	2hEr!Er!zEzE	horizons	hErai′zEnz
h	1horEorEzAzA	horizontal	ho″rEzA′ntEl
h	1horEorEzAzA	horizontally	ho″rEzA′ntElli
h	1hormrm%n=nØ	hormone	ho′rmou″n
h	1hormrm%nzzØ	hormones	ho′rmou″nz
h	1hornrnØ====	horn	horn
h	1hornrnØ====	Horne	horn
h	1hornnzØ====	horns	hornz
h	1horEorEwIwI	Horowitz	ho′rEwI″ts
h	1horEorEbEbE	horrible	ho′rEbEl
h	1horEorEbEbE	horribly	ho′rEbElli
h	1horEorEf!f!	horrified	ho′rEfai″d
h	1horEorEf!f!	horrifying	ho′rEfai″IN
h	1hor*or*r=rØ	horror	ho′r*r
h	1hor*or*rzzØ	horrors	ho′r*rz
h	1horsrsØ====	horse	hors
h	1horsrsEz=zØ	horse's	ho′rsEz
h	1horssbak=kØ	horseback	ho′rsba″k
h	1horssmEnSSI	horsemanship	ho′rsmEnSI″p
h	1horssmEn=nØ	horsemen	ho′rsmEn
h	1horspl$==$Ø	horseplay	ho′rsplei″
h	2horssp@r=rØ	horsepower	ho′rspau″r
h	1horsrsEz=zØ	horses	ho′rsEz
h	1horsrsEz=zØ	horses'	ho′rsEz
h	1h%z=%zØ====	hose	houz
h	1h%zE%zEz=zØ	hoses	hou′zEz
h	2hAspspItEtE	hospitable	hAspI′tEbEl
h	1hAspspItEtE	hospital	hA′spI″tEl
h	1hAspspEtata	hospitality	hA″spEta′lEti

h	1hAspspItEtE	hospitalization	hA"spItElEzei'SEn
h	1hAspspItEtE	hospitals	hA'spI"tElz
h	1h%ststØ====	host	houst
h	1h%sttsØ====	host's	housts
h	1hAststIj=jØ	hostage	hA'stIj
h	1h%ststEs=sØ	hostess	hou'stEs
h	1h%ststEsEsE	hostesses	hou'stEsEz
h	1hAststEl=lØ	hostile	hA'stEl
h	2hAststIlElE	hostilities	hAstI'lEtiz
h	2hAststIlElE	hostility	hAstI'lEti
h	1h%sttsØ====	hosts	housts
h	1hAt=AtØ====	hot	hAt
h	1hAtStSAt=tØ	hot-shot	hA'tSA"t
h	2h%te%tel=lØ	hotel	houte'l
h	2h%te%telzzØ	hotels	houte'lz
h	1hAtltli==iØ	hotly	hA'tli
h	1hAt*At*r=rØ	hotter	hA't*r
h	1hAtEAtEsttØ	hottest	hA'tEst
h	1hEf=EfØ====	Hough	hEf
h	1h%tE%tEn=nØ	Houghton	hou'tEn
h	1h@k=@kØ====	Houk	hauk
h	1h@ndndØ====	hound	haund
h	1h@nddzØ====	hounds	haundz
h	1h@s=@sØ====	house	haus
h	1h@s=@sØ====	House	haus
h	1h@z=@zØ====	house	hauz
h	1h@zdzdØ====	housed	hauzd
h	1h@shsh%lddØ	household	hau'shou"ld
h	1h@shsh%ldd*	householder	hau'shou"ld*r
h	1h@shsh%ldzØ	households	hau'shou"ldz
h	1h@skskip*p*	housekeeper	hau'ski"p*r
h	1h@skskipIpI	housekeeping	hau'ski"pIN
h	1h@zE@zEz=zØ	houses	hau'zEz
h	1h@swsw!f=fØ	housewife	hau'swai"f
h	1h@swsw!vzzØ	housewives	hau'swai"vz

h	1h@swsw*rkkØ	housework	hau'sw*"rk
h	1h@zI@zIN=NØ	housing	hau'zIN
h	1h@smsmEnzzØ	Housman's	hau'smEnz
h	1yustEn=nØ	Houston	hyu'stEn
h	1hEvEEvEl=lØ	hovel	hE'vEl
h	1hEv*Ev*r=rØ	hover	hE'v*r
h	1h@==h@Ø====	how	hau
h	1h@d=@dØ====	how'd	haud
h	1h@z=@zØ====	how's	hauz
h	1h@rdrdØ====	Howard	hau'rd
h	1h@==h@Ø====	Howe	hau
h	1h@evh@ev*v*	however	hau"e'v*r
h	1h@l=@lØ====	howl	haul
h	1h@lI@lIN=NØ	howling	hau'lIN
h	1h@lzlzØ====	howls	haulz
h	1h#t=#tØ====	Hoyt	hoit
h	1yub*ub*rttØ	Hubert	hyu'b*rt
h	1hEbzbzØ====	hubs	hEbz
h	1hEksst*r=rØ	huckster	hE'kst*r
h	1hEdEEdEl=lØ	huddle	hE'dEl
h	1hEdEEdElddØ	huddled	hE'dEld
h	1hEdEEdElIlI	huddling	hE'dElIN
h	1hEdsdsEn=nØ	Hudson	hE'dsEn
h	1hEdsdsEnzzØ	Hudson's	hE'dsEnz
h	1yu==yuØ====	hue	hyu
h	1hEg=EgØ====	hug	hEg
h	1yuj=ujØ====	huge	hyuj
h	1hEgdgdØ====	hugged	hEgd
h	1hEgIEgIN=NØ	hugging	hE'gIN
h	1yu==yuØ====	Hugh	hyu
h	1yuz=uzØ====	Hughes	hyuz
h	1hE==hEØ====	huh	hE
h	1hElklkØ====	hulk	hElk
h	1hElklkIN=NØ	hulking	hE'lkIN
h	1hElkksØ====	hulks	hElks

h	1hEl=El∅====	hull	hEl
h	1hEm=Em∅====	hum	hEm
h	1yumEumEn=n∅	human	hyu'mEn
h	2yumumn=n∅	humane	hyumei'n
h	1yumEumEnInI	humanism	hyu'mEnI"zEm
h	1yumEumEnEnE	humanist	hyu'mEnEst
h	1yumEumEnInI	humanistic	hyu"mEnI'stIk
h	2yumaumanEnE	humanitarian	hyuma"nEte'riEn
h	2yumaumanEnE	humanities	hyuma'nEtiz
h	2yumaumanEnE	humanity	hyuma'nEti
h	1yumEumEnnnE	humanness	hyu'mEnnEs
h	1yumEumEnzz∅	humans	hyu'mEnz
h	1hEmbmbEl=l∅	humble	hE'mbEl
h	1hEmbmbElll i	humbly	hE'mbElli
h	1yum=um∅====	Hume	hyum
h	2yumIumIdEdE	humidity	hyumI'dEti
h	2yumIumIlili	humiliated	hyumI'liei"tEd
h	2yumIumIlili	humiliating	hyumI'liei"tIN
h	2yumIumIlili	humiliation	hyumI"liei'SEn
h	2yumIumIlElE	humility	hyumI'lEti
h	1hEmdmd∅====	hummed	hEmd
h	1hEmIEmIN=N∅	humming	hE'mIN
h	1hEmEEmEkss∅	hummocks	hE'mEks
h	1yum*um*r=r∅	humor	hyu'm*r
h	1yum*um*rErE	humorous	hyu'm*rEs
h	1hEmffri==i∅	Humphrey	hE'mfri
h	1hEncnc∅====	hunch	hEnc
h	1hEncct∅====	hunched	hEnct
h	1hEnddrEd=d∅	hundred	hE'ndrEd
h	1hEnddrEdAdA	hundred-odd	hE'ndrEdA"d
h	1hEnddrEdzz∅	hundreds	hE'ndrEdz
h	1hEnddrEdTT∅	hundredth	hE'ndrEdT
h	1hEN=EN∅====	hung	hEN
h	2hENgNgeriri	Hungarian	hENge'riEn
h	1hENgNg*riri	Hungary	hE'Ng*ri

h	1hENgNg*r=rØ	hunger	hE'Ng*r
h	1hENgNg*riri	hungry	hE'Ng*ri
h	1hENkNkØ====	hunk	hENk
h	1hENkNk*rddØ	hunkered	hE'Nk*rd
h	1hEntntØ====	hunt	hEnt
h	1hEntntØ====	Hunt	hEnt
h	1hEntntEd=dØ	hunted	hE'ntEd
h	1hEntnt*r=rØ	hunter	hE'nt*r
h	1hEntnt*r=rØ	Hunter	hE'nt*r
h	1hEntnt*rkkI	hunter-killer	hE'nt*rkI"l*r
h	1hEntnt*rzzØ	hunters	hE'nt*rz
h	1hEntntIN=NØ	hunting	hE'ntIN
h	1hEnttli==iØ	Huntley	hE'ntli
h	1hEnttsØ====	hunts	hEnts
h	1h*rdrdEl=lØ	hurdle	h*'rdEl
h	1h*rlrlØ====	hurl	h*rl
h	1h*rlldØ====	hurled	h*rld
h	1h*rlrlIN=NØ	hurling	h*'rlIN
h	1y*rA*rAk=kØ	Hurok	hy*'rA"k
h	2hErAErA==AØ	hurrah	hErA'
h	1h*rE*rEkk	hurricane	h*'rEkei"n
h	1h*ri*rid=dØ	hurried	h*'rid
h	1h*rE*rEdlli	hurriedly	h*'rEdli
h	1h*ri*ri==iØ	hurry	h*'ri
h	1h*ri*riINiI	hurrying	h*'riIN
h	1h*rtrtØ====	hurt	h*rt
h	1h*rtrtIN=NØ	hurting	h*'rtIN
h	1h*rtrtElIlI	hurtling	h*'rtElIN
h	1h*rttsØ====	hurts	h*rts
h	1hEzbzbEnddØ	husband	hE'zbEnd
h	1hEzbzbEndzØ	husband's	hE'zbEndz
h	1hEzbzbEndri	husbandry	hE'zbEndri
h	1hEzbzbEndzØ	husbands	hE'zbEndz
h	1hES=ESØ====	hush	hES
h	1hEStStØ====	hushed	hESt

h	1hEskski==iØ	husky	hE'ski
h	1hEsEEsEl=lØ	hustle	hE'sEl
h	1hEsEEsEldd Ø	hustled	hE'sEld
h	1hEsEEsEl*l*	hustler	hE'sEl*r
h	1hEt=EtØ====	hut	hEt
h	1hEcEEcEnzzØ	Hutchins	hE'cEnz
h	1hEtstsØ====	huts	hEts
h	1hEtEEtEn=nØ	Hutton	hE'tEn
h	1hEkssli==iØ	Huxley	hE'ksli
h	1hEkssliz=zØ	Huxley's	hE'ksliz
h	2h!anh!anEnE	Hyannis	haia'nEs
h	1h!drdr!d=dØ	hydride	hai'drai"d
h	1h!drdr%kAkA	hydrocarbon	hai"droukA'rbEn
h	1h!drdrEjEjE	hydrogen	hai'drEjEn
h	1h!ji!jin=nØ	hygiene	hai'ji"n
h	1hIm=ImØ====	hymn	hIm
h	1hImzmzØ====	hymns	hImz
h	1h!p*!p*rbbA	hyperbolic	hai"p*rbA'lIk
h	1h!fE!fEnn	hyphenated	hai'fEnei"tEd
h	2hEpAEpAkrrE	hypocrisies	hEpA'krEsiz
h	2hEpAEpAkrrE	hypocrisy	hEpA'krEsi
h	1hIpEIpEkrrI	hypocrite	hI'pEkrI"t
h	1hIpEIpEkrrI	hypocrites	hI'pEkrI"ts
h	1h!p%!p%TaTa	hypothalamus	hai"pouTa'lEmEs
h	2h!pA!pATETE	hypotheses	haipA'TEsiz
h	2h!pA!pATETE	hypothesis	haipA'TEsEs
h	2h!pA!pATETE	hypothesized	haipA'TEsai"zd
h	1h!pE!pETeTe	hypothetical	hai"pETe'tEkEl
h	2hIststeriri	hysteria	hIste'riE
h	2hIststerErE	hysterical	hIste'rEkEl
j	2h%z$%z$==$Ø	Jose	houzei'
wh	1hu==huØ====	who	hu
wh	1hud=udØ====	who'd	hud
wh	1huz=uzØ====	who's	huz
wh	1huevhuev*v*	whoever	hu"e'v*r

wh	lh%l=%lØ====	whole	houl
wh	lh%lsls$l=lØ	wholesale	hou'lsei"l
wh	lh%lslsEm=mØ	wholesome	hou'lsEm
wh	lh%llli==iØ	wholly	hou'lli
wh	lh%llli%ni%	wholly-owned	hou'lliou"nd
wh	lhum=umØ====	whom	hum
wh	lhupIupIN=NØ	whooping	hu'pIN
wh	lhor=orØ====	whore	hor
wh	lhuz=uzØ====	whose	huz
wh	lhus%us%ev%e	whosoever	hu"soue'v*r

3. Categorical Determination of /b,p/ in English

outcomes: /b/, /p/

variables:

7 intervals of time measuring voicing onset time (VOT)

each interval 7 msec long, from +2 msec to +51 msec

data set (outcome, variables, VOT):

b	xxxxxxx	-107	p	ooooooo	51
b	xxxxxxx	-97	p	ooooooo	51
b	xxxxxxx	-83	p	ooooooo	63
b	xxxxxxx	-71	p	ooooooo	63
b	xxxxxxx	-58	p	ooooooo	63
b	xxxxxxx	-53	p	ooooooo	63
b	xxxxxxx	-49	p	ooooooo	70
b	xxxxxxx	-48	p	ooooooo	70
b	xxxxxxx	-32	p	ooooooo	71
b	xxxxxxx	-19	p	ooooooo	71
b	xxxxxxx	0	p	ooooooo	73
b	xxxxxxx	0	p	ooooooo	73
b	xxxxxxx	0	p	ooooooo	83
b	xxxxxxx	1	p	ooooooo	83
b	xxxxxxx	1	p	ooooooo	83
b	xxxxxxx	1	p	ooooooo	83
b	xxxxxxx	1	p	ooooooo	88
b	xxxxxxx	2	p	ooooooo	88
b	xxxxxxx	2	p	ooooooo	94
b	xxxxxxx	2	p	ooooooo	94

4. Terms of Address in Colloquial Egyptian Arabic

outcomes: *ya'axi, yaxuuya* (both meaning 'my brother')

variables:

1 speaker sex (**f**emale, **m**ale)

2 speaker social class (**l**ower, **m**iddle, **u**pper)

3 speaker age (**m**iddle-aged, **o**ld, **y**oung)

4 addressee social class (**l**ower, **m**iddle, **u**pper)

5 addressee age (**m**iddle-aged, **o**ld, **y**oung)

6 speaker's tone of voice (**n**egative, **p**ositive)

7 power relationship of speaker to addressee (**d**ominant, **e**qual, **s**ubordinate)

8 closeness of speaker and addressee (**n**uclear family, **f**riend, **k**nown, **r**elative, **u**nknown)

data set (variables, outcome, frequency):

flmlmneu	yaxuuya	2
flmlmpef	yaxuuya	1
flmlmpeu	yaxuuya	1
flmlopef	yaxuuya	1
flmlyneu	yaxuuya	1
flmlyper	yaxuuya	1
flmmopef	yaxuuya	1
flmmopeu	yaxuuya	1
flmmyneu	yaxuuya	1
flolmneu	yaxuuya	1
flolmpef	yaxuuya	1
flolopeu	yaxuuya	1
flolyndn	ya'axi	1
	yaxuuya	1
flolyneu	yaxuuya	2
flomypeu	yaxuuya	1
flylmnef	yaxuuya	1
flylmpeu	yaxuuya	1
flylopsn	yaxuuya	1
flylynef	yaxuuya	1
flylyner	yaxuuya	1
flylypeu	yaxuuya	1
flymmpeu	yaxuuya	1
flyumpeu	yaxuuya	1

fmmlmneu	yaxuuya	1
fmmmyndn	ya'axi	1
fmomonsn	ya'axi	2
fmomyndn	yaxuuya	1
fmouyneu	yaxuuya	1
fmymmneu	yaxuuya	1
fmymonsn	ya'axi	2
fmymynef	ya'axi	2
fmymyner	ya'axi	1
	yaxuuya	1
fumuonsn	yaxuuya	1
fuoloneu	yaxuuya	1
fuolynek	yaxuuya	1
fuouyndn	ya'axi	1
	yaxuuya	1
fuouypsn	yaxuuya	1
fuyumnef	ya'axi	1
fuyuynef	yaxuuya	4
fuyuyner	ya'axi	2
	yaxuuya	6
fuyuyper	yaxuuya	1
mlmlmnek	ya'axi	1
	yaxuuya	1
mlmlmneu	ya'axi	1
mlmlmpef	ya'axi	1
	yaxuuya	2
mlmlmpeu	yaxuuya	1
mlmlonef	ya'axi	1
mlmlonek	ya'axi	1
mlmlopeu	yaxuuya	1
mlmlyndn	ya'axi	1
mlmlynef	yaxuuya	1
mlmlynek	yaxuuya	1
mlmlyneu	ya'axi	1
	yaxuuya	1

mlmlypef	yaxuuya	2
mlmlypek	yaxuuya	1
mlmmmneu	ya'axi	1
mlmmmpeu	yaxuuya	1
mlmmoneu	yaxuuya	1
mlmmypsk	yaxuuya	2
mlmuynsu	ya'axi	1
mlolmnek	ya'axi	1
mloloneu	ya'axi	1
mlolyndk	ya'axi	1
mlolynef	ya'axi	2
mlolynef	yaxuuya	1
mlolynek	yaxuuya	1
mlolypef	ya'axi	1
mlommpef	yaxuuya	1
mlommpeu	ya'axi	1
mlomyneu	ya'axi	1
	yaxuuya	1
mlylonef	yaxuuya	1
mlylynef	ya'axi	8
	yaxuuya	2
mlylynek	yaxuuya	1
mlylyner	ya'axi	1
mlylyneu	ya'axi	1
mlylypef	ya'axi	3
	yaxuuya	2
mlylyper	ya'axi	1
mlymynef	ya'axi	4
mlymyneu	ya'axi	1
mlymypef	yaxuuya	1
mlyuynsu	yaxuuya	1
mmmlmpef	ya'axi	1
mmmlmpeu	ya'axi	2
mmmlonek	ya'axi	1
mmmlopeu	yaxuuya	1

mmmlyndk	ya'axi	1
mmmlyneu	ya'axi	1
mmmlypdk	yaxuuya	1
mmmmmnef	ya'axi	1
	yaxuuya	1
mmmmmnek	ya'axi	1
mmmmmneu	yaxuuya	1
mmmmmpef	ya'axi	1
	yaxuuya	1
mmmmmpeu	yaxuuya	1
mmmmyndn	ya'axi	2
mmmmynek	ya'axi	1
mmmmyner	ya'axi	2
mmmmypef	yaxuuya	1
mmmumneu	yaxuuya	1
mmmuynsk	ya'axi	1
mmolmneu	yaxuuya	1
mmoloneu	ya'axi	1
mmolypef	ya'axi	1
mmommnef	ya'axi	1
mmomypef	yaxuuya	1
mmomypsk	yaxuuya	1
mmoumneu	yaxuuya	1
mmylynek	yaxuuya	1
mmylyneu	ya'axi	1
mmymmndu	yaxuuya	1
mmymmnef	ya'axi	1
mmymynef	ya'axi	18
	yaxuuya	7
mmymyner	ya'axi	1
mmymynsu	ya'axi	1
mmymypef	ya'axi	6
	yaxuuya	3
mmymypeu	ya'axi	1
mmyuyneu	ya'axi	1
mumlmneu	yaxuuya	1
mumlynek	yaxuuya	1
mummmpeu	ya'axi	1
mumumnef	ya'axi	2
mumumneu	ya'axi	1
mumuyndn	ya'axi	1
muolmneu	ya'axi	1
muouonef	ya'axi	1
muouoner	yaxuuya	1
muouyper	ya'axi	1
muylmndk	ya'axi	1
	yaxuuya	1
muyuynef	ya'axi	13
	yaxuuya	5
muyuynek	ya'axi	1
muyuyner	ya'axi	4
muyuyneu	ya'axi	1
	yaxuuya	1
muyuypef	ya'axi	5
	yaxuuya	4
muyuyper	yaxuuya	1

5. Past Tense in Finnish

(restricted to two-syllable verb stems ending in *a, ä,* or *e*)

outcomes: *V-i, a-oi, tV-si, hte-ksi*

variables:

1 the word-initial phoneme

2 the first vowel in the word

3 whether the first vowel is immediately followed by another vowel in the same syllable (V) or not (ø)

4 the following vowel in the same syllable, if it exists (see the third variable); if not, the non-specification symbol (=)

5 whether the vowel(s) of the first syllable are followed by a sonorant in the same syllable (S) or not (ø)

6 the following sonorant in the same syllable, if it exists (see the fifth variable); if not, the non-specification symbol (=)

7 whether the vowel(s) of the first syllable are followed by an obstruent in the same syllable (O) or not (ø)

8 the following obstruent in the same syllable, if it exists (see the seventh variable); if not, the non-specification symbol (=)

9 the last consonant in the word

10 the last vowel in the word

data set (verb stem, gloss, variables, current outcome, original outcome [if different from current outcome]):

```
aja     drive                aaØ=Ø=Ø=ja  a-oi
alka    begin                aaØ=SlØ=ka  a-oi
anta    give                 aaØ=SnØ=ta  a-oi
```

autta	help	aaVuØ=Otta	a-oi	
elä	live	eeØ=Ø=Ø=lä	V-i	
estä	prevent	eeØ=Ø=Ostä	V-i	
haasta	summon	haVaØ=Osta	a-oi	
haise	smell [intran.]	haViØ=Ø=se	V-i	
haista	smell [tran.]	haViØ=Osta	a-oi	
hake	go get	haØ=Ø=Ø=ke	V-i	
heittä	throw	heViØ=Ottä	V-i	
hiihtä	ski	hiViØ=Ohtä	V-i	
hohta	gleam	hoØ=Ø=Ohta	V-i	
hoita	tend	hoViØ=Ø=ta	V-i	tV-si
huolta	maintain	huVoSlØ=ta	tV-si	
huuta	shout	huVuØ=Ø=ta	tV-si	
ime	suck	iiØ=Ø=Ø=me	V-i	
iske	strike	iiØ=Ø=Oske	V-i	
itke	cry	iiØ=Ø=Otke	V-i	
itä	germinate	iiØ=Ø=Ø=tä	V-i	tV-si
jaka	divide	jaØ=Ø=Ø=ka	a-oi	
jaksa	have strength	jaØ=Ø=Oksa	a-oi	
jatka	continue	jaØ=Ø=Otka	a-oi	
jauha	grind	jaVuØ=Ø=ha	a-oi	
johta	lead	joØ=Ø=Ohta	V-i	
jousta	be flexible	joVuØ=Osta	V-i	
juokse	run	juVoØ=Okse	V-i	
jättä	leave (behind)	jäØ=Ø=Ottä	V-i	
jäytä	gnaw	jäVyØ=Ø=tä	V-i	tV-si
kaata	overturn	kaVaØ=Ø=ta	a-oi	
kaihta	shun	kaViØ=Ohta	a-oi	
kaiva	dig	kaViØ=Ø=va	a-oi	
kanta	carry	kaØ=SnØ=ta	a-oi	
kartta	avoid	kaØ=SrOtta	a-oi	
kasva	grow	kaØ=Ø=Osva	a-oi	
katta	roof	kaØ=Ø=Otta	a-oi	
keittä	cook	keViØ=Ottä	V-i	
kestä	last	keØ=Ø=Ostä	V-i	

kieltä	forbid	kiVeSlØ=tä	tV-si	
kiertä	wind	kiVeSrØ=tä	tV-si	
kiistä	dispute	kiViØ=Ostä	V-i	
kiittä	thank	kiViØ=Ottä	V-i	
kiitä	speed	kiViØ=Ø=tä	V-i	tV-si
kitke	weed (out)	kiØ=Ø=Otke	V-i	
koitta	dawn	koViØ=Otta	V-i	
koke	experience	koØ=Ø=Ø=ke	V-i	
koske	touch	koØ=Ø=Oske	V-i	
kosta	get revenge	koØ=Ø=Osta	V-i	
kulke	move (forward)	kuØ=SlØ=ke	V-i	
kuole	die	kuVoØ=Ø=le	V-i	
kuule	hear	kuVuØ=Ø=le	V-i	
kuulta	shine faintly	kuVuSlØ=ta	tV-si	
kylpe	take a bath	kyØ=SlØ=pe	V-i	
kylvä	sow	kyØ=SlØ=vä	V-i	
kyntä	plow	kyØ=SnØ=tä	V-i	tV-si
kyte	smolder	kyØ=Ø=Ø=te	V-i	tV-si
kytke	tie (up)	kyØ=Ø=Otke	V-i	
käske	command	käØ=Ø=Oske	V-i	
kätke	hide	käØ=Ø=Otke	V-i	
käyttä	use	käVyØ=Ottä	V-i	
kääntä	turn	käVäSnØ=tä	tV-si	
laitta	prepare	laViØ=Otta	a-oi	
laske	let go	laØ=Ø=Oske	V-i	
laula	sing	laVuØ=Ø=la	a-oi	
lentä	fly	leØ=SnØ=tä	tV-si	
liittä	join	liViØ=Ottä	V-i	
loista	shine	loViØ=Osta	V-i	
luista	glide	luViØ=Osta	V-i	
luke	read	luØ=Ø=Ø=ke	V-i	
luotta	trust	luVoØ=Otta	V-i	
luule	suppose	luVuØ=Ø=le	V-i	
lähte	depart	läØ=Ø=Ohte	V-i	hte-ksi
löytä	find	löVyØ=Ø=tä	tV-si	

mahta	be capable of	maØ=Ø=Ohta	a-oi	
maista	taste	maViØ=Osta	a-oi	
maksa	pay	maØ=Ø=Oksa	a-oi	
maltta	have patience	maØ=SlOtta	a-oi	
mene	go	meØ=Ø=Ø=ne	V-i	
muista	remember	muViØ=Osta	V-i	
murta	break	muØ=SrØ=ta	tV-si	
muutta	change	muVuØ=Otta	V-i	
myöntä	admit	myVöSnØ=tä	tV-si	
naura	laugh	naVuØ=Ø=ra	a-oi	
niele	swallow	niVeØ=Ø=le	V-i	
niittä	mow	niViØ=Ottä	V-i	
nosta	lift	noØ=Ø=Osta	V-i	
nouse	rise	noVuØ=Ø=se	V-i	
nouta	fetch	noVuØ=Ø=ta	V-i	tV-si
nyhtä	pull (out)	nyØ=Ø=Ohtä	V-i	
nylke	skin	nyØ=SlØ=ke	V-i	
näke	see	näØ=Ø=Ø=ke	V-i	
näyttä	show	näVyØ=Ottä	V-i	
ole	be	ooØ=Ø=Ø=le	V-i	
osta	buy	ooØ=Ø=Osta	V-i	
otta	take	ooØ=Ø=Otta	V-i	
paahta	scorch	paVaØ=Ohta	a-oi	
paina	weigh	paViØ=Ø=na	a-oi	
paista	bake	paViØ=Osta	a-oi	
pala	burn	paØ=Ø=Ø=la	a-oi	
pane	put	paØ=Ø=Ø=ne	V-i	
peittä	cover (up)	peViØ=Ottä	V-i	
pese	wash	peØ=Ø=Ø=se	V-i	
pettä	deceive	peØ=Ø=Ottä	V-i	
piekse	whip	piVeØ=Okse	V-i	
piile	be hidden	piViØ=Ø=le	V-i	
piirtä	draw	piViSrØ=tä	tV-si	
pistä	sting	piØ=Ø=Ostä	V-i	
pitä	hold	piØ=Ø=Ø=tä	V-i	tV-si

poista	remove	poViØ=Osta	V-i	
polke	trample (on)	poØ=SlØ=ke	V-i	
poltta	burn	poØ=SlOtta	V-i	
pote	be sick	poØ=Ø=Ø=te	V-i	tV-si
puke	dress	puØ=Ø=Ø=ke	V-i	
pure	bite	puØ=Ø=Ø=re	V-i	
purka	unloose	puØ=SrØ=ka	V-i	
puske	butt	puØ=Ø=Oske	V-i	
pyytä	request	pyVyØ=Ø=tä	tV-si	
pyörtä	turn back	pyVöSrØ=tä	tV-si	
pääse	get somewhere	päVäØ=Ø=se	V-i	
päästä	let go	päVäØ=Ostä	V-i	
päättä	decide	päVäØ=Ottä	V-i	
raasta	grate	raVaØ=Osta	a-oi	
rientä	hasten	riVeSnØ=tä	tV-si	
riistä	deprive	riViØ=Ostä	V-i	
riittä	be enough	riViØ=Ottä	V-i	
ryöstä	rob	ryVöØ=Ostä	V-i	
saatta	accompany	saVaØ=Otta	a-oi	
sata	rain	saØ=Ø=Ø=ta	a-oi	
sietä	tolerate	siVeØ=Ø=tä	V-i	tV-si
siirtä	move	siViSrØ=tä	tV-si	
soitta	ring	soViØ=Otta	V-i	
sotke	make a mess	soØ=Ø=Otke	V-i	
souta	row	soVuØ=Ø=ta	V-i	tV-si
suista	hurl	suViØ=Osta	V-i	
sula	melt	suØ=Ø=Ø=la	V-i	
sulke	close	suØ=SlØ=ke	V-i	
sure	grieve	suØ=Ø=Ø=re	V-i	
syyttä	accuse	syVyØ=Ottä	V-i	
syytä	toss	syVyØ=Ø=tä	V-i	tV-si
syökse	plunge	syVöØ=Okse	V-i	
syöttä	feed	syVöØ=Ottä	V-i	
särke	shatter	säØ=SrØ=ke	V-i	
säästä	save	säVäØ=Ostä	V-i	

säätä	enact	säVäØ=Ø=tä	V-i	tV-si
taita	know how	taViØ=Ø=ta	tV-si	a-oi
taitta	break (in two)	taViØ=Otta	a-oi	
tappa	kill	taØ=Ø=Oppa	a-oi	
teettä	have made	teVeØ=Ottä	V-i	
teke	do	teØ=Ø=Ø=ke	V-i	
tietä	know	tiVeØ=Ø=tä	tV-si	
toista	repeat	toViØ=Osta	V-i	
tuke	support	tuØ=Ø=Ø=ke	V-i	
tule	come	tuØ=Ø=Ø=le	V-i	
tunke	force	tuØ=SNØ=ke	V-i	
tunte	feel	tuØ=SnØ=te	tV-si	
tuotta	produce	tuVoØ=Otta	V-i	
työntä	push	tyVöSnØ=tä	tV-si	
täyttä	fill	täVyØ=Ottä	V-i	
uitta	float	uuViØ=Otta	V-i	
vaihta	(ex)change	vaViØ=Ohta	a-oi	
vala	cast (metal)	vaØ=Ø=Ø=la	a-oi	
vetä	pull	veØ=Ø=Ø=tä	V-i	tV-si
viettä	spend (time)	viVeØ=Ottä	V-i	
viistä	brush (past)	viViØ=Ostä	V-i	
virkka	utter	viØ=SrOkka	a-oi	
voitta	win	voViØ=Otta	V-i	
vuole	carve	vuVoØ=Ø=le	V-i	
vuota	leak	vuVoØ=Ø=ta	V-i	tV-si
vyöttä	gird (up)	vyVöØ=Ottä	V-i	
väittä	argue	väViØ=Ottä	V-i	
välttä	avoid	väØ=SlOttä	V-i	
vääntä	twist	väVäSnØ=tä	tV-si	
yltä	reach	yyØ=SlØ=tä	V-i	tV-si

Appendix Three

PASCAL PROGRAM

```
{written in Turbo Pascal, version 3.0
   (Turbo Pascal is a registered trademark of Borland International)

determines the analogical set for Fasold's data
   (see section 4.3 of text)

runs on 8088 microprocessor with 640 KB RAM
   and 20 MB hard disk

two input files (CONSDEL.DAT, CONSDEL.OUT)
   and one output file (CONSDEL.PRD)

constants at beginning of program
   set according to format of input files}


program analogy;
   {for a given context determines the analogical set
      and predicts the outcome for that context}
```

```
var
  file_description : string[8];
  i, j, k : integer;
  space : char;
  data_file, outcome_file : text;
  num_data : integer;
const
  {number of items in <file_description>.DAT}
    data_size = 370;
  {number of outcomes in <file_description>.OUT}
    num_outcome = 2;
  {number of variables in <file_description>.DAT}
    num_var = 3;
  {2**num_var - 1}
    num_cntxt = 7;
  {(num_dat - 1) div 256}
    num_set = 1;
  {maximum length of data specification}
    data_spec_length = 5;
  {maximum length of outcome specification}
    outcome_spec_length = 11;
type
  data_type = record
                remembered : boolean;
                outcome : char;
                variables : string[num_var];
                spec : string[data_spec_length];
                freq : real
              end;
  outcome_type = record
                   outcome : char;
                   spec : string[outcome_spec_length];
                   freq : real
                 end;
```

```
var
  data : array[1..data_size] of data_type;
  outcome : array[1..num_outcome] of outcome_type;
const
  null = '=';
var
  outfile : text;
  quit, exclude_given, exclude_null : boolean;
  ch : char;
  given_variables : string[num_var];
var
  active_var, active_context : integer;
  var_set : set of 1..num_var;
type
  set_pointer = ^sets;
  sets = array[0..num_set] of set of 0..255;
  context_type = record
                   code : char;
                   data_set : set_pointer
                 end;
var
  context : array[0..num_cntxt] of context_type;
  offset, twos_power : integer;
  set_index, set_place : integer;
  new_context : boolean;
  upper : integer;
  freq : real;
  data_block : integer;
  position : integer;
  data_number : integer;
  total_freq : real;
  percent : integer;
  probability : real;
  number : integer;
  count : integer;
  random_count : integer;
```

```
  average : array[1..num_outcome] of real;
  sum : array[1..num_outcome] of real;
  predictable : integer;
  percentage : real;
  total_sum : real;

begin

  {select the parameters}

  clrscr;
  file_description := 'CONSDEL';
  write('Give the probability ');
  write('that data will be remembered: ');
  readln(probability);
  writeln;
  write('Give the number of tests ');
  write('for Monte Carlo estimation: ');
  readln(number);

  {read in the data set}

  assign(data_file, file_description + '.DAT');
  reset(data_file);
  i := 0;
  while not eof(data_file) do
  begin
    i := i + 1;
    readln(data_file, data[i].outcome,
      space, data[i].variables, space, data[i].spec)
  end;
  close(data_file);

  assign(outcome_file, file_description + '.OUT');
  reset(outcome_file);
  i := 0;
```

```
while not eof(outcome_file) do
begin
  i := i + 1;
  readln(outcome_file, outcome[i].outcome,
    space, outcome[i].spec)
end;
close(outcome_file);

assign(outfile, file_description + '.PRD');
rewrite(outfile);

{read in the given context}

writeln;
write('                                    ');
for i := 1 to num_var do
  write(i mod 10);
writeln;
write('Specify the given context (', num_var:2, ' variables): ');
  readln(given_variables);
writeln(outfile, 'GIVEN CONTEXT: ', given_variables);
writeln(outfile);
writeln(outfile, '  probability = ', probability:6:5);
writeln(outfile);
writeln(outfile, '  number of Monte Carlo tests = ', number);
writeln(outfile);
writeln;

{set the parameters for the given context}

write('Do you want to exclude this context from the data? ');

write('(Y/N) ');
read(kbd, ch);
exclude_given := upcase(ch) = 'Y';
```

```
if exclude_given then
begin
  writeln(outfile, '  given excluded from the data set');
  writeln(outfile);
  writeln('yes')
end
else
begin
  writeln(outfile, '  given included in the data set');
  writeln(outfile);
  writeln('no')
end;
if pos(null, given_variables) <> 0 then
begin
  writeln;
  write('Do you want to exclude null variables? (Y/N) ');
  read(kbd, ch);
  exclude_null := upcase(ch) = 'Y';
  if exclude_null then
  begin
    writeln('yes');
    writeln(outfile, '  null variables excluded');
    writeln(outfile)
  end
  else
  begin
    writeln('no');
    writeln(outfile, '  null variables included');
    writeln(outfile)
  end
end
else exclude_null := false;

{determine which items in the data set are remembered}

writeln(outfile);
```

```
writeln;
num_data := data_size;
predictable := 0;
for i := 1 to num_outcome do
begin
  sum[i] := 0;
  average[i] := 0
end;
for count := 1 to number do
begin
  randomize;
  for i := 1 to data_size do
    data[i].remembered := random < probability;
  for i := 1 to num_data do
    data[i].freq := 0;
  for i := 1 to num_outcome do
    outcome[i].freq := 0;
  for i := 0 to num_cntxt do
  begin
    context[i].code := '0';
    context[i].data_set := nil
  end;

  active_var := 0;
  active_context := 1;
  var_set := [];
  for i := 1 to num_var do
  begin
    if (not exclude_null)
      or (given_variables[i] <> null) then
    begin
      active_var := active_var + 1;
      active_context := active_context shl 1;
      var_set := var_set + [i]
    end
  end;
```

```
{set up the contextual space}

random_count := 0;
for i := 1 to num_data do
begin
  if data[i].remembered then
  begin
    random_count := random_count + 1;
    if (not exclude_given)
      or (given_variables <> data[i].variables) then
    begin
      offset := 0;
      twos_power := 1;
      for j := 1 to num_var do
      begin
        if j in var_set then
        begin
          if given_variables[j] <> data[i].variables[j] then
            offset := offset + twos_power;
          twos_power := twos_power shl 1
        end
      end;
      new_context := false;
      with context[offset] do
      begin
        case code of
          '0' : begin
                  code := data[i].outcome;
                  new_context := true
                end;
          'A'..'Z', 'a'..'z' : if code <> data[i].outcome then
                                 code := '1'
        end;
        set_index := (i - 1) div 256;
        set_place := (i - 1) mod 256;
```

```
        if new_context then
        begin
          new(data_set);
          for j := 0 to num_set do
            data_set^[j] := []
        end;
        data_set^[set_index] := data_set^[set_index] + [set_place]
      end
    end;
  end
end;

{test for homogeneity}

for i := 0 to (active_context - 1) do
begin
  if context[i].code <> '0' then
  begin
    upper := i;
    twos_power := 1;
    for j := 1 to active_var do
    begin
      if upper mod 2 = 0 then
      begin
        if context[i].code = '1' then
        begin
          if context[i+twos_power].code = '0' then
          begin
            context[i+twos_power].code := '1';
            new(context[i+twos_power].data set);
            for k := 0 to num_set do
              context[i+twos_power].data_set^[k] :=
                context[i].data_set^[k]
          end
          else context[i+twos_power].code := '2'
        end
```

```
        else
          if context[i].code = '2' then
            context[i+twos_power].code := '2'
          else
            if context[i+twos_power].code
              = context[i].code then
              for k := 0 to num_set do
                context[i+twos_power].data_set^[k] :=
                  context[i+twos_power].data_set^[k] +
                    context[i].data_set^[k]
            else
              if context[i+twos_power].code = '0' then
              begin
                context[i+twos_power].code := context[i].code;
                new(context[i+twos_power].data_set);
                for k := 0 to num_set do
                  context[i+twos_power].data_set^[k] :=
                    context[i].data_set^[k]
              end
              else
                context[i+twos_power].code := '2';
      end;
      twos_power := twos_power shl 1;
      upper := upper shr 1;
    end
  end
end;

{create the analogical set}

for i := 0 to (active_context - 1) do
begin
  if not(context[i].code in ['0', '2']) then
  begin
    freq := 0;
```

```
    for set_index := 0 to num_set do
      if context[i].data_set^[set_index] <> [] then
        for set_place := 0 to 255 do
          if set_place in context[i].data_set^[set_index]
            then freq := freq + 1;
    for set_index := 0 to num_set do
      if context[i].data_set^[set_index] <> [] then
      begin
        data_block := set_index * 256;
        for set_place := 0 to 255 do
          if set_place in context[i].data_set^[set_index]
          then
          begin
            data_number := data_block + set_place + 1;
            data[data_number].freq := data[data_number].freq + freq
          end
      end
  end
end;

{count the frequencies in the analogical set}

for i := 1 to num_data do
begin
  if data[i].freq <> 0 then
  begin
    position := ord(data[i].outcome);
    if position < 91 then
      position := position - 64
    else position := position - 70;
    outcome[position].freq :=
      outcome[position].freq + data[i].freq
  end
end;

total_freq := 0;
```

```
for i := 1 to num_outcome do
begin
  if outcome[i].freq <> 0 then
    total_freq := total_freq + outcome[i].freq
end;

{print out the results}

writeln(outfile, count, ' ANALOGICAL SET');
writeln(outfile);
writeln(outfile, '  total frequency = ', total_freq:1:0);
writeln(outfile);

writeln(count, ' ANALOGICAL SET');
writeln;
writeln('  total frequency = ', total_freq:1:0);
writeln;

for i := 1 to num_data do
begin
  if data[i].freq <> 0 then
  begin
    percent := round(1000 * (data[i].freq/total_freq));
    writeln(outfile, '  ', data[i].outcome, ' ',
      data[i].spec:data_spec_length, ' ',
      data[i].freq:10:0, ' ', percent:4);
    writeln('  ', data[i].outcome, ' ',
      data[i].spec:data_spec_length, ' ',
      data[i].freq:10:0, ' ', percent:4)
  end
end;

writeln(outfile);
writeln;
```

```
  writeln(outfile, '  number of items remembered = ',
           random_count:3, ' (out of ', data_size:3, ')');
  writeln(outfile);

  for i := 1 to num_outcome do
  begin
    if outcome[i].freq <> 0 then
    begin
      percent := round(1000 * (outcome[i].freq/total_freq));
      percentage := 1000 * (outcome[i].freq/total_freq);
      writeln(outfile, '  ', outcome[i].outcome, ' ',
        outcome[i].spec:outcome_spec_length, ' ',
        outcome[i].freq:10:0, ' ', percent:4);
      writeln('  ', outcome[i].outcome, ' ',
        outcome[i].spec:outcome_spec_length, ' ',
        outcome[i].freq:10:0, ' ', percent:4);
      sum[i] := sum[i] + percentage
    end
  end;

  writeln(outfile);

  if random_count <> 0 then
    predictable := predictable + 1;

  writeln(outfile);
  writeln;

  for i := 0 to num_cntxt do
    if context[i].data_set <> nil then
      dispose(context[i].data_set);

end;

writeln(outfile);
writeln;
```

```
  writeln(outfile, 'SUMMARY');
  writeln('SUMMARY');
  writeln(outfile, '  number of predictable cases: ', predictable);
  writeln('  number of predictable cases: ', predictable);
  total_sum := 0;
  if predictable <> 0 then
  begin
    for i := 1 to num_outcome do
      total_sum := total_sum + sum[i];
    for i := 1 to num_outcome do
    begin
      average[i] := 1000 * sum[i]/total_sum;
      writeln(outfile, '  average for outcome ', outcome[i].outcome, ' = ',
        average[i]:5:0);
      writeln('  average for outcome ', outcome[i].outcome, '=',
        average[i]:5:0)
    end
  end;
  close(outfile)

end.
```

CONSDEL.DAT (re-arranged into columns)

```
A vwp vwp1        B vwp vwp8        B vwp vwp15
A vwp vwp2        B vwp vwp9        B vwp vwp16
A vwp vwp3        B vwp vwp10       B vwp vwp17
A vwp vwp4        B vwp vwp11       B vwp vwp18
A vwp vwp5        B vwp vwp12       B vwp vwp19
A vwp vwp6        B vwp vwp13       B vwp vwp20
B vwp vwp7        B vwp vwp14       B vwp vwp21
```

```
B vwp vwp22
B vwp vwp23
B vwp vwp24
B vwp vwp25
B vwp vwp26
B vwp vwp27
B vwp vwp28
B vwp vwp29
B vwp vwp30
B vwp vwp31
B vwp vwp32
B vwp vwp33
B vwp vwp34
B vwp vwp35
B vwp vwp36
B vwp vwp37
B vwp vwp38
B vwp vwp39
B vwp vwp40
B vwp vwp41
B vwp vwp42
B vwp vwp43
B vwp vwp44
B vwp vwp45
B vwp vwp46
B vwp vwp47
B vwp vwp48
B vwp vwp49
B vwp vwp50
B vwp vwp51
B vwp vwp52
B vwp vwp53
B vwp vwp54
B vwp vwp55
B vwp vwp56
B vwp vwp57
B vwp vwp58
B vwp vwp59
B vwp vwp60
B vwp vwp61
B vwp vwp62
B vwp vwp63
B vwp vwp64
B vwp vwp65
B vwp vwp66
B vwp vwp67
A vwf vwf1
A vwf vwf2
A vwf vwf3
A vwf vwf4
A vwf vwf5
A vwf vwf6
A vwf vwf7
A vwf vwf8
A vwf vwf9
A vwf vwf10
A vwf vwf11
A vwf vwf12
A vwf vwf13
B vwf vwf14
B vwf vwf15
B vwf vwf16
B vwf vwf17
B vwf vwf18
B vwf vwf19
B vwf vwf20
B vwf vwf21
B vwf vwf22
B vwf vwf23
B vwf vwf24
B vwf vwf25
B vwf vwf26
B vwf vwf27
B vwf vwf28
B vwf vwf29
B vwf vwf30
B vwf vwf31
B vwf vwf32
B vwf vwf33
B vwf vwf34
B vwf vwf35
B vwf vwf36
B vwf vwf37
B vwf vwf38
B vwf vwf39
B vwf vwf40
B vwf vwf41
B vwf vwf42
B vwf vwf43
B vwf vwf44
B vwf vwf45
B vwf vwf46
B vwf vwf47
B vwf vwf48
B vwf vwf49
B vwf vwf50
B vwf vwf51
B vwf vwf52
B vwf vwf53
B vwf vwf54
B vwf vwf55
A vws vws1
A vws vws2
A vws vws3
A vws vws4
```

A vws vws5
A vws vws6
A vws vws7
A vws vws8
A vws vws9
A vws vws10
A vws vws11
A vws vws12
A vws vws13
A vws vws14
A vws vws15
B vws vws16
B vws vws17
B vws vws18
B vws vws19
B vws vws20
B vws vws21
B vws vws22
B vws vws23
B vws vws24
B vws vws25
B vws vws26
B vws vws27
B vws vws28
B vws vws29
B vws vws30
B vws vws31
B vws vws32
B vws vws33
B vws vws34
B vws vws35
B vws vws36
B vws vws37
B vws vws38
B vws vws39
B vws vws40
B vws vws41
B vws vws42
B vws vws43
B vws vws44
B vws vws45
B vws vws46
B vws vws47
B vws vws48
B vws vws49
B vws vws50
B vws vws51
B vws vws52
B vws vws53
B vws vws54
B vws vws55
B vws vws56
B vws vws57
B vws vws58
B vws vws59
B vws vws60
B vws vws61
B vws vws62
B vws vws63
A vmp vmp1
A vmp vmp2
A vmp vmp3
A vmp vmp4
A vmp vmp5
A vmp vmp6
A vmp vmp7
A vmp vmp8
A vmp vmp9
A vmp vmp10
A vmp vmp11
A vmp vmp12
B vmp vmp13
B vmp vmp14
A vmf vmf1
A vmf vmf2
B vmf vmf3
B vmf vmf4
B vmf vmf5
A vms vms1
A vms vms2
A vms vms3
A vms vms4
A vms vms5
A vms vms6
A vms vms7
B vms vms8
B vms vms9
B vms vms10
B vms vms11
B vms vms12
A cwp cwp1
A cwp cwp2
A cwp cwp3
A cwp cwp4
A cwp cwp5
A cwp cwp6
A cwp cwp7
A cwp cwp8
A cwp cwp9
A cwp cwp10
A cwp cwp11
A cwp cwp12
A cwp cwp13
A cwp cwp14
A cwp cwp15

```
A cwp cwp16
A cwp cwp17
A cwp cwp18
A cwp cwp19
A cwp cwp20
A cwp cwp21
A cwp cwp22
B cwp cwp23
B cwp cwp24
B cwp cwp25
B cwp cwp26
B cwp cwp27
B cwp cwp28
B cwp cwp29
B cwp cwp30
B cwp cwp31
B cwp cwp32
B cwp cwp33
B cwp cwp34
B cwp cwp35
A cwf cwf1
A cwf cwf2
A cwf cwf3
A cwf cwf4
A cwf cwf5
A cwf cwf6
A cwf cwf7
A cwf cwf8
A cwf cwf9
A cwf cwf10
A cwf cwf11
A cwf cwf12
A cwf cwf13
A cwf cwf14
A cwf cwf15
A cwf cwf16
A cwf cwf17
A cwf cwf18
A cwf cwf19
A cwf cwf20
A cwf cwf21
A cwf cwf22
A cwf cwf23
A cwf cwf24
B cwf cwf25
B cwf cwf26
B cwf cwf27
B cwf cwf28
B cwf cwf29
B cwf cwf30
B cwf cwf31
B cwf cwf32
A cws cws1
A cws cws2
A cws cws3
A cws cws4
A cws cws5
A cws cws6
A cws cws7
A cws cws8
A cws cws9
A cws cws10
A cws cws11
A cws cws12
A cws cws13
A cws cws14
A cws cws15
A cws cws16
A cws cws17
A cws cws18
A cws cws19
A cws cws20
A cws cws21
A cws cws22
A cws cws23
A cws cws24
A cws cws25
A cws cws26
A cws cws27
A cws cws28
A cws cws29
A cws cws30
A cws cws31
A cws cws32
A cws cws33
A cws cws34
A cws cws35
A cws cws36
A cws cws37
B cws cws38
B cws cws39
B cws cws40
B cws cws41
B cws cws42
B cws cws43
B cws cws44
B cws cws45
B cws cws46
B cws cws47
A cmp cmp1
A cmp cmp2
A cmf cmf1
A cmf cmf2
A cmf cmf3
A cmf cmf4
```

```
A cmf cmf5
A cmf cmf6
A cmf cmf7
A cmf cmf8
A cmf cmf9
A cmf cmf10
A cmf cmf11
B cmf cmf12
B cmf cmf13
A cms cms1
A cms cms2
A cms cms3
A cms cms4
A cms cms5
A cms cms6
A cms cms7
A cms cms8
A cms cms9
A cms cms10
A cms cms11
A cms cms12
A cms cms13
A cms cms14
A cms cms15
A cms cms16
A cms cms17
A cms cms18
A cms cms19
A cms cms20
A cms cms21
B cms cms22
B cms cms23
B cms cms24
B cms cms25
```

CONSDEL.OUT

```
A deleted
B not deleted
```

INDEX